Jossey-Bass Teacher

Jossey-Bass Teacher provides educators with practical knowledge and tools to create a positive and lifelong impact on student learning. We offer classroom-tested and research-based teaching resources for a variety of grade levels and subject areas. Whether you are an aspiring, new, or veteran teacher, we want to help you make every teaching day your best. From ready-to-use classroom activities to the latest teaching framework, our value-packed books provide insightful, practical, and comprehensive materials on the topics that matter most to K–12 teachers. We hope to become your trusted source for the best ideas from the most experienced and respected experts in the field.

Differentiated Instruction for the Middle School Science Teacher

Activities and Strategies for an Inclusive Classroom

Joan D'Amico and Kate Gallaway

Foreword by Dorothy Lozauskas Sherwood

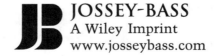

JOSSEY-BASS
A Wiley Imprint
www.josseybass.com

Illustrations by Alice Beresin

Jossey-Bass books and products are available through most bookstores. To contact Jossey-Bass directly call our Customer Care Department within the U.S. at 800-956-7739, outside the U.S. at 317-572-3986, or fax 317-572-4002.

Jossey-Bass also publishes its books in a variety of electronic formats. Some content that appears in print may not be available in electronic books.

Image on page 112 is taken from *Art Explosion: 250,000 Images*.

ISBN: 9780787984670

Printed in the United States of America

FIRST EDITION

PB Printing   10 9 8 7 6 5 4 3

Contents

Part One: Being Successful in the Inclusive Classroom

Part Two: Science Activities for the Inclusive Middle School Classroom

About This Book

The goal of this book is to help middle school science teachers effectively teach the wide range of students found in their classrooms. Science is a balance between the vast amount of content knowledge and the process of scientific investigation. Middle school science is an important foundation for students because there is an emphasis on different disciplines at each grade level. Teachers strive to provide students with the core concepts, principles, and theories of science. Students can then build upon and investigate these in more depth in high school. Teachers must deliver instruction in a variety of ways to ensure that there is a balance between procedures and creative problem solving. It can be tricky to accomplish this with a class filled with students of varying learning styles and skill levels. This book is the practical, easy-to-use answer to this problem. It approaches science concepts the way you do, as a middle school teacher, and helps you find an effective way to present the material to the whole class. Then it shows how to guide practice while also modifying the material to provide access to the same content standard for all your students. Just as important, it helps you find ways to involve students' families and tie the science concepts into their everyday lives. Relevance is a powerful motivator. Through such methods as incorporating technology, science becomes relevant to the needs of the middle school student in the twenty-first century. The conversational style and thoroughness of this book make it easy to start using it right away.

Here's what you will find in this book. In Part One, Chapter One focuses on successful collaboration with the school team and with parents and families. There are several checklists to help streamline the process. Chapter Two focuses on assessing students' learning styles to differentiate instruction. There are several different ways to assess your students so that you can choose the learning styles that best fit you and your classroom. Finally, Chapter Three focuses on tips for successful instruction in the inclusive classroom, including alternative assessment techniques.

The activities in Part Two conform to national content standards, and they are specially designed to help you differentiate instruction for your inclusive classroom. The activities appeal to a wide range of learning styles and abilities, all within individual lessons. A list of supplies is given at the beginning of each activity. Then each activity walks you through a lesson for presenting a traditional lesson to the whole class. You have several options when it comes to making the notes accessible to all students: you can make transparencies to use on the overhead, scan them into your computer to project using an LCD or interactive whiteboard, or make copies for individual students.

Each lesson is followed by a worksheet designed to review and reinforce the concepts presented in the lesson. Students may complete the worksheet "as is," or you may use it as a pretest to define various levels of student understanding. There is also an exciting, hands-on component included with each activity, the Whole Class Lab. These labs provide students with an opportunity to really see the scientific concepts in action. Because these are labs, they require more time and materials, so it is up to you whether or not to use any given one. The lessons can stand alone without the labs.

Understanding safe science practices is a key piece in understanding science itself, and safety must be taught. A science laboratory can and should be a safe place to perform experiments. Students can prevent accidents if they think about what they are doing at all times, use good judgment, observe safety rules, and follow directions. Here are some general laboratory safety procedures:

- Wear eye protection when working on experiments.
- Do not eat or drink while in the laboratory.
- Do not taste any chemical.
- Long hair must be tied back so it will not fall into chemicals or flames.
- Follow directions and wait for permission to begin.
- Wipe all counter surfaces and hands with soap and water.
- Never point the open end of a test tube at yourself or another person.
- If you want to smell a substance, do not hold it directly to your nose. Instead, hold the container a few centimeters away and use your hand to fan vapors toward you.
- Flush the sink with large quantities of water when disposing of liquid chemicals or solutions.

The *Science Safety Handbook for California Public Schools* was created to help science teachers understand and avoid situations in which accidents might occur in the science laboratories or on field trips and outdoor education experiences. It can be accessed through the California Department of Education at www.cde.ca.gov/pd/ca/sc/documents/scisafebk.pdf.

Each activity includes a section, "How to Adapt This Lesson for the Inclusive Classroom," that offers a variety of teaching strategies, methods, and tools to use after you have separated the class into appropriate stations to differentiate instruction. These stations include a multitude of modalities offered to remediate, reinforce, or enrich the concepts presented.

Another section, titled "Home/School Connection," can be used to invite parents to be a part of the learning process. Activities here are family based, and include life skills and practical learning.

At the end of each activity, we've given some suggestions for assessment of the skills presented. These activities can be used as an integral component of the science curriculum or as a supplement to the chosen textbook. The format can be adapted to the individual middle school teacher's curriculum needs.

About the Authors

Joan D'Amico, M.A., is a learning disabilities teacher/consultant in the Garfield School District in New Jersey and has a private practice as a learning disabilities specialist. While teaching middle school for seven years in Wayne, New Jersey, she won the New Jersey Governor's Teaching for Excellence Award. In addition, she has taught workshops in elementary and middle schools, as well as conducted seminars in the business sector for teachers and students teaching academic concepts using multisensory activities. She has appeared on CNN, TNN, and the Food Network. D'Amico is a member of the New Jersey Association of Learning Consultants and the American Federation of Teachers (AFT).

She is also a coauthor of a series of seven books published by John Wiley & Sons that focuses on teaching academic subjects using food and cooking, creative experiments, and multisensory activities. Among them are *The Science Chef, The Math Chef, The Healthy Body Cookbook,* and *The Coming to America Cookbook.* With Kate Gallaway, she has coauthored *Differentiated Instruction for the Middle School Math Teacher,* and *Differentiated Instruction for the Middle School Language Arts Teacher.* She is currently pursuing a doctorate in teacher leadership.

Kate Gallaway, M.A., is an instructor at Chapman University in Monterey, California, teaching science and math methods to beginning teachers and graduate students. She frequently makes public appearances across the country at conferences and to different parent groups. She also has a private practice in Carmel, California, specializing in math and study skills, and she has worked with children of all ages. She is an educational therapist with a B.A. in psychology from UCLA and a master's in mild to moderate learning disabilities from San Francisco State University, where she also earned her educational therapist certification. She is a credentialed teacher and the coauthor of the book *Managing the Mathematics Classroom.* With Joan D'Amico, she has coauthored *Differentiated Instruction for the Middle School Math Teacher,* and *Differentiated Instruction for the Middle School Language Arts Teacher.*

This book is dedicated to our children,
Christi, Alexa, and Kyle D'Amico and Grant and Pierce Gallaway,
for making it "all worthwhile."

Acknowledgments

We wish to thank the following individuals:

- Our parents, Joseph Lange and Mary and Richard Lind, for being a lifelong source of inspiration and motivation.
- Husband Ralph D'Amico, for his intellect, eternal fountain of knowledge, ideas, and support.
- Husband Wally Gallaway, for his confidence in me and unwavering support.
- Our editor, Kate Bradford, for believing in this project from the beginning.
- Friend Anthony Rufo, for his constant encouragement and willingness to help out at all times and without question.
- Ms. Dorothy Sherwood, for her wisdom, science expertise, and manuscript review.
- Ms. Fran D'Amico, for her science knowledge and support.
- The wonderful colleagues and friends at Garfield Middle School and the Garfield Child Study Team (Garfield, New Jersey), and Schuyler-Colfax Middle School (Wayne, New Jersey), who generously gave input and ideas when needed.
- To the students and their families who served as inspiration through their hard work and commitment to learning. You have greatly touched our lives.

Foreword

Teaching middle school children presents myriad challenges for every teacher. The children are experiencing rapid changes in their physical appearance, hormone-driven emotional responses to daily occurrences, and ever-changing relationships with their peers. Additionally, children mature at different rates, read at different grade levels, possibly possess disabilities, and have unique personalities. When you add to this list the push to excel in academics, sports, and the arts, it is readily apparent that the middle school child truly requires the very best teaching strategies specifically designed for this age group!

My own career in education has spanned three decades in New Jersey, in the roles of Verona Public Schools science teacher, Mountain Lakes district supervisor of curriculum and instruction for science and mathematics, and Wayne middle school principal. Throughout these years, I have always been an advocate of hands-on science activities that require the students to develop their higher-order thinking skills. Students need time to think about scientific concepts in inquiry-based laboratory experiments and time to share their ideas with a partner or in groups. The goal is to move the student's thinking from a knowledge base of information to the application level, and beyond to the "What if . . . ?" questions and synthesis level of Bloom's Taxonomy of the Cognitive Domain. Middle school students are definitely able to attain this goal when provided with such learning activities as those in *Differentiated Instruction for the Middle School Science Teacher: Activities and Strategies for an Inclusive Classroom*.

Within every middle school classroom are students with a wide array of developmental levels, disabilities, reading levels, and interests. As a science teacher, I always found it a daunting task to meet the needs of every child and provide the tools for each of them to attain his or her personal best. Having a resource book of suggested teaching activities that effectively address these varied needs would have helped a great deal, and it has now been written by Joan D'Amico and Kate Gallaway. *Differentiated Instruction for the Middle School Science Teacher* is a step-by-step resource book of lesson plans designed to fit into a typical forty-minute class period. The plans include suggested questions that "set the stage for learning" the specific topic of the day, detailed directions for setting up the planned activity, worksheets for the students, small-group activities, and specific ideas for the evaluation of the student's knowledge and understanding. This book includes creative homework assignments that both reinforce the subject matter and extend the student's comprehension. These "Home/School Connection" ideas truly serve as bridges between the science lesson and activity in the classroom and creating a positive working relationship with the student's family.

The lesson plans in this valuable resource book span all the areas of middle school science: life science, physical science, and earth science. In each lesson, the authors include extended enrichment activities for the gifted students, and specific strategies for helping the learning disabled students, delayed readers, those with fine motor or perceptual difficulties, and those with cognitive impairments.

Differentiated Instruction for the Middle School Science Teacher is a resource that every middle school science teacher will appreciate. It is "user-friendly" for the teacher, because it meets the varied and challenging educational needs of our twenty-first-century students. This book should be part of every science teacher's "toolbox of lesson plans"!

December 2009

Dorothy Lozauskas Sherwood
Principal
Schuyler-Colfax Middle School
Wayne, New Jersey

Part One

Being Successful in the Inclusive Classroom

Chapter 1

Collaborating Effectively

Success in the inclusive classroom is due in large part to collaboration with others in the school. Teaching an inclusive classroom is difficult to do alone, and there are systems in place so that you don't have to. In this chapter, we look at some general ways of making collaboration work for you.

Collaborating for Intervention

All teachers are eager to communicate information to all of their students. If a student is struggling with classroom performance or cannot understand the material presented in class, then you need to assist and monitor this student to try to help him or her. This chapter focuses on what to do when this approach fails: how to help students when the work continues to be difficult, even after extra assistance has taken place, and there has to be an intervention.

Often a teacher will ask, "What do I do with a student who is having difficulties learning in my class? How can I get him or her help? Do I need to request an evaluation to see if special education is necessary?"

Teachers often bring this topic of discussion to a member of the Child Study Team for advice. A Child Study Team is a group of specialists who are trained to determine if a child has a learning disability. The team is primarily made up of a psychologist, a learning specialist, and a social worker. The first question that the Child Study Team should pose is, "What prereferral intervention strategies have been implemented, and what was the student outcome?"

Prereferral intervention strategies are generally determined by a committee of general education teachers before any specialists are included in the plan. The committee's job is to try to assist students who are failing subjects within the confines of the general education setting. The student's main subject teachers, along with the guidance counselor, meet to discuss what can be changed in the classroom setting to enhance student progress. Typical prereferral intervention strategies at the middle school level can include these:

- Changing the student's seat
- Calling parents for a conference
- Talking with the student
- Assigning the student to a "study buddy"
- Changing the student's teacher
- Placing the student on a weekly behavioral progress sheet, signed by parents and teachers
- Placing the student on a weekly homework modification sheet, signed by parents and teachers
- Suggesting after-school assistance or tutoring
- Deciding if the student should attend basic skills classes
- Retention

The teachers then agree to implement specific modifications, deciding on a meeting date to monitor the child's progress and determine if the outcome was positive. If progress is not being made, a referral to the Child Study Team may be warranted.

A checklist can be a helpful aid in determining a clear plan of action. This information can be stored in the student's permanent record folder (see next page).

Collaborating with the Child Study Team

Establishing positive relationships with all members of the school is important. In an inclusive classroom, open lines of communication between the general and special education teachers, as well as with support personnel, are essential for a thorough understanding of all students' learning needs. Discussions with past and present teachers, as well as a complete record review, can give the middle school teacher insight into planning for students in the inclusive classroom. The Child Study Team can be an excellent resource for further information on a particular student's special needs. The members of the team can also offer assistance in implementing modifications and learning strategies set forth by an Individual Education Program (IEP). An IEP is a document that explains a plan of action and program tailored to a student's specific learning and behavioral needs. This is a legal document. It's contents must be agreed on by the child's parents or guardians and implemented in school by the teachers.

Checklist for Prereferral Interventions

Name: _____   Date: _____

Reason for meeting: _____

_____

_____

Fill in the following prereferral interventions to be implemented and monitored:

Intervention	Person Responsible	Date Implemented
Calls to parents		
Changing student's seat in the classroom		
Interview with student		
Student visit to guidance counselor		
Parent conference		
Suggestions for after-school assistance or tutoring		
Assigning a study buddy		
Assigning a weekly behavioral progress sheet, signed by parents and teachers		
Recommendation for basic skills or compensatory assistance		
Retention		
Additional classroom interventions		

Comments: _____

_____

_____

_____

Follow-up meeting date: _____

Members of the Child Study Team

The core specialists on the Child Study Team are a psychologist, an education therapist, and a social worker. (A speech and language specialist is also part of the core team, but only for preschool students.) These individuals are trained in the diagnosis and remediation of learning disabilities. The team may also include additional professionals who can offer classroom strategies and home suggestions, such as special and general education teachers, school nurses and other staff, speech and motor therapists, paraprofessionals, and the child's parents.

School Psychologist

In many states, the school psychologist is the main support person responsible for assessing the learning levels of students who are referred to the Child Study Team. He or she can do this through standardized and nonstandardized assessments that measure learning strengths and weaknesses. The most popular tool used by the school psychologist is an individual Intelligence Quotient (IQ) test. The IQ test, an accepted measure of intellectual functioning nationwide, offers one way to assess students' verbal and nonverbal abilities. The assessment is administered individually and is completed in approximately one two-hour session.

The school psychologist may also assess the student's academic levels in mathematics, reading, written language, and oral language, as well as learning styles and strengths and weaknesses, through specific diagnostic standardized testing instruments, functional assessments, report card grades, teacher interviews, classroom observations, and past standardized test performance.

Finally, the school psychologist assesses any emotional and behavioral concerns that may impede the learning process. This evaluation can be accomplished through interviews with the student, teachers, and parents, as well as using scales and instruments designed to measure these adaptive functions.

The Learning Disabilities Teacher/Consultant or Educational Therapist (LDT/C or Educational Diagnostician)

Not all states have an LDT/C or educational therapist as part of their school teams. The main roles of this person as a team member are to complete psychoeducational testing to determine the student's academic strengths and weaknesses and develop remedial modifications to aid in therapeutically teaching the student with disabilities. The LDT/C can also do what a psychologist does as part of the Child Study Team. He or she measures specific levels in mathematics, reading, and written and oral language, and then develops skills and strategies to be used in the classroom for remediation.

School Social Worker

The school social worker is responsible for obtaining student and family background information and determining if the child's home life now or in the past is having an impact on his or her educational performance. Family, birth, and developmental history are obtained through an interview with the parents. School social workers also can help students during times of impending or actual individual or school crisis.

Speech and Language Therapists

The job of the speech and language therapist on the Child Study Team is to determine if a student's articulation and language abilities are standing in the way of the child's learning success in school. Through standardized and functional assessment tools, these therapists can determine if the child has weaknesses in phonology, syntax, articulation, or written language. If they diagnose a communication disorder, the Child Study Team can prescribe individual, group, or collaborative therapy.

Special Education Teachers

Special education teachers are trained to teach skills and strategies for remediation purposes and are in part responsible for implementing the educational modifications designated in IEPs. They are knowledgeable in working with students with learning disabilities and can be essential as support teachers, along with paraprofessionals, in the inclusive classroom.

General Education Teachers

General education teachers in the middle school environment are teachers who specialize in one area of the curriculum, such as English, history, math, reading, or science. They collaborate with special education teachers and paraprofessionals to communicate their subject matter effectively to all students in an inclusive classroom. This is accomplished by cooperative planning and development of pretests, worksheets, learning strategies, study guides, modifications, and reviews.

School Nurse

The school nurse is required to complete vision and hearing screenings and check attendance, as well as offer specific nursing services to special and general education students. These services can include administering medications, changing catheters, checking hearing devices, storing wheelchairs, and monitoring blood pressure and sugar levels.

Guidance Counselors

Guidance counselors work as liaisons with the teachers, students, parents, administration, and school team. They arrange prereferral meetings with the teachers to identify and determine intervention strategies for students who are struggling in the general education environment. They also make sure that prereferral interventions are executed and outcomes are monitored. Guidance counselors are responsible for administering standardized tests, recording grades, and monitoring all students. In a middle school environment, it is not unusual to have a guidance counselor assigned to each grade level.

School Administration

Principals, vice principals, and deans of students are part of the school administration. An ongoing relationship between classroom teachers and the school administration is essential when identifying students with learning disabilities or emotional and behavioral difficulties, because these professionals are often the first people to address consequences stemming from the manifestations of student problems in the classroom. The principals and student deans are usually responsible for assigning detentions, suspensions, and expulsions from school.

Physical Therapists

Physical therapists evaluate and provide therapies to strengthen gross motor skills. They provide these services in an individual, small-group, or natural setting according to their own and the Child Study Team's recommendations. Recently there has been an increase in administering therapies in a natural setting, such as the school hallway. For a student who needs strength walking in a natural setting, the therapist walks with the student during passing time. A natural setting does not change or contrive the environment for therapy.

Occupational Therapists

Occupational therapists evaluate and provide therapies to strengthen fine motor and organizational skills. In a younger child, individual therapy often seeks to strengthen hand and finger muscles, correct pencil grip, and help the child gain motor control while writing. For older students, occupational therapists are brought in to help enhance students' written expression and organizational skills. These services are provided in an individual, small-group, or natural setting.

Paraprofessionals

Paraprofessionals, part of the school team in an inclusive classroom, assist the teacher in implementing both group and individual lesson plans. They collaborate with the teacher on strategies and ideas, mark papers, teach small-group lessons, reinforce and review information presented in class, and arrange materials for small-station instruction. They also perform many routine classroom duties, such as collecting and organizing class assignments, homework, and projects.

Personal Aides

Personal aides can be part of a special education student's IEP. The personal aide's role is to assist assigned students with specific personal needs related to the school environment, such as those who may need additional assistance navigating a building with a wheelchair or with a walker, or using an elevator. The checklist on the next page will help teachers determine with whom to confer first.

Referral Interventions

Sometimes teachers can have great success with minimal modifications within the general education classroom setting. At other times, the learning or behavioral difficulties are too severe, and students continue to do poorly in spite of prereferral intervention strategies. If this is determined, a follow-up meeting may be scheduled to discuss the possibilities of a referral to the Child Study Team. If possible Child Study Team services have been decided on at this meeting, a referral form is then filled out by one or more teachers to be addressed by the Intervention and Referral Services Committee (I&RS).

The IRS includes at least one general and one special education teacher, the guidance counselor, and one member of the Child Study Team. The referring teacher brings information on current classroom performance, grades, and results of the prereferral intervention strategies that were implemented for the child in question. The committee, with the help of the Child Study Team representative, decides if a team evaluation is warranted at this time.

Prereferral Collaboration with School Personnel Checklist

Teachers who encounter problem situations do not always know whom to ask for assistance or advice. Complete the exercise below to test your own knowledge of personnel roles and resources.

With Whom Should I Confer First?

Use the information that has been presented so far in this chapter and advice from your own Child Study Team to determine the best person to speak to first regarding initial concerns about a student. Read through the following situations and use the list of abbreviations at the end of the list to mark each concern with the appropriate person to talk to.

_____ Andrew may need to go to summer school, or retaining him seems evident.

_____ Joshua has difficulties completing math homework, and his grade average for the marking period will be lower as a result.

_____ In spite of several intervention strategies, Tyler has difficulties with reading comprehension skills.

_____ Eric sits in the back of the classroom all day and doesn't make eye contact with anyone. He is not completing his work.

_____ Brianna broke her leg and needs a key to the elevator.

_____ Aisha has severe headaches and needs medication at lunchtime in school.

_____ Sarah was caught cheating during a midterm exam.

_____ Elle, a new student with spina bifida, needs additional exercises added to her program.

_____ Part of a new program involves setting up station materials for students to learn math in different modalities.

_____ Alex needs a study guide for an upcoming social studies test.

_____ Michael's handwriting looks very labored and resembles that of a much younger child.

_____ Several students were upset after the unexpected death of a classmate.

_____ Last year in sixth grade, Juan did well in science, but this year he is failing the class.

List of Abbreviations

Psy = School psychologist	Para = Paraprofessional
LDT/C = Learning consultant or educational therapist	Gui = Guidance counselor
Soc = School social worker	Adm = Administration
OT = Occupational therapist	Spec = Special education teacher
PT = Physical therapist	Gen = General education teacher
SN = School Nurse	

The Case Manager

If the I&RS decides that a Child Study Team evaluation might be warranted, a person on the team who is designated to be the case manager contacts the parents. Throughout the evaluation process, the case manager has these responsibilities:

- Facilitating communication between the parents and the school staff
- Communicating with the guidance counselor and teachers
- Understanding the student's learning strengths and weaknesses in the classroom
- Becoming knowledgeable of the student's abilities, home circumstances, and ongoing progress in school throughout the evaluation
- Understanding and implementing time lines for prompt completion of evaluations and for program eligibility as mandated by state and federal law

At this point, the case manager sends a formal written letter to the student's parents stating that a meeting has been scheduled to discuss their child's progress and a possible Child Study Team evaluation.

The Planning Meeting

During the planning meeting, the core team of specialists must be present, along with the referring teacher and parent. If the child shows apparent weaknesses in speech and language or is receiving English as a Second Language (ESL) services, the speech and language therapist may also be invited. (Speech and language specialists must be present for younger students; this is optional at the middle school level.) At this meeting, the parent and referring teacher voice their concerns, and an evaluation plan is determined based on the scope of the problem.

At least two evaluations, to be completed by core team members, must be recommended to set the process in motion. The specialists may recommend some of these evaluations:

- *Educational evaluation.* Administered by the educational therapist, LDT/C, or psychologist, this evaluation assesses the student's learning strengths and weaknesses, assesses the student's academic level, and identifies his or her learning styles.
- *Psychological evaluation.* Administered by the school psychologist, this evaluation primarily assesses basic aptitude and abilities as related to school performance. Adaptive behavior can be evaluated using a variety of scales to determine the child's emotional and behavioral states.
- *Developmental history.* This is completed by the school social worker in an interview with the parent to determine the child's birth and developmental history, as well as address pertinent family concerns.
- *Speech and language evaluation.* Administered by the speech and language therapist, this evaluation assesses the child's articulation and oral and written language.

These evaluations are generally completed by a core member of the Child Study Team. At the planning meeting, the members may determine that other evaluations are warranted—for example:

- *Physical therapy evaluation.* This is completed by a physical therapist, usually hired by the school system to assess the child's gross motor skills.

- *Occupational therapy evaluation.* Completed by an occupational therapist, usually hired by the school system, this evaluation assesses hand strength, fine motor abilities, self-help skills, written expression, and organizational skills.
- *Psychiatric evaluation.* Usually completed by an outside psychiatrist, this evaluation is recommended for students with severe behavioral or emotional concerns.
- *Vision and hearing screening.* The initial screening is completed by the school nurse. If a problem is detected, the nurse then refers the student to an ophthalmologist or audiologist.
- *Neurological evaluation.* An evaluation of the neurological system is usually completed by an outside neurologist. Students with severe attention or focusing concerns may be referred by the team to a neurologist to determine the root cause of this difficulty.
- *Audiological evaluation.* This is an outside evaluation, usually recommended for students with symptoms of severe language processing disorders.
- *Technology evaluation.* This evaluation, completed by an outside specialist, determines if any technological equipment, such as an augmentative device for speaking or an FM system for hearing, may be necessary to aid in an appropriate education for the student.

The Evaluation Process

Once the evaluation has begun, the team collaborates and collects and interprets results from the evaluations. The case manager is the facilitator in coordinating all information necessary to determine the child's eligibility for a special education program. Guidelines and time lines for the evaluation process are mandated by state laws.

When all the reports are collected, the team decides whether the student is eligible for special services and if a learning disability exists. An eligibility meeting is held with the parents to determine classification. Once the parent signs the eligibility document, an IEP is designed to address the student's learning strengths and weaknesses through placement, skills, strategies, subject levels, and classroom modifications. The program is measured yearly through the development of goals and objectives. The case manager monitors the program.

All students with disabilities are entitled to a free and appropriate education according to the Individuals with Disabilities Act (IDEA), a federal law passed in 1975. A free and appropriate education must take place in the least restrictive environment (LRE) and be designed to address each student's unique and special needs. These provisions for special education and related services including parental and student rights, are valid from ages three to twenty-one. This evaluation process is illustrated in Figure 1.1, and page 12 provides teachers with a step-by-step checklist to guide them in the referral process.

Figure 1.1

Evaluations are completed

▼

Evaluations are collected and interpreted by the team to determine eligibility

▼

An eligibility meeting with the parents is called

▼

Parents sign eligibility document

▼

An IEP is designed

▼

The program is measured using yearly goals/objectives

Checklist for Referring a
Student to the School Team

As a classroom teacher, have I completed the following?

- ☐ Met with the prereferral intervention team?

- ☐ Implemented interventions over an appropriate and mutually decided length of time?

- ☐ Documented the lack of intervention progress?

- ☐ Filled out a referral sheet?

- ☐ Brought information to the I&RS committee chairperson?

- ☐ Attended an IRS meeting with information completed on the referral sheet and presented the information to the committee?

Notes

_____

_____

_____

_____

_____

_____

_____

_____

_____

_____

_____

_____

_____

Collaborating with Parents and Families

Part of a teacher's professional success relies on building a strong, open communication line between the home and school. A positive connection between home and school increases the overall success of a child's learning.

It is imperative to empower all parents by helping them realize that they are an integral part of their child's education. Parents can offer important insights into their child's study habits, behaviors, past homework history, health, sleep patterns, and general personality characteristics. These factors, which may not be readily apparent in the classroom environment, can have an impact on achievement for both general education and special needs students.

Research on student success in school found that participation in educational activities at home had a positive influence on school success. Results suggest that enhancing parental involvement in a child's schooling relates to overall improved school performance. One reason may be that parents of higher-achieving students set higher standards for their children's educational activities than do parents of low-achieving students.

Encouraging Parental Involvement

Family participation in a child's education is more predictive of a student's academic success than socioeconomic status. Parental involvement can lead to:

- Higher grades
- Higher test scores
- Better attention
- Increased motivation
- Lower rate of suspension
- Decreased use of drugs and alcohol
- Fewer instances of violent behavior
- Higher self-esteem

Parents may have to become a bit more creative in their types of involvement as the child enters middle school. However, parental involvement at this level is just as important as in the earlier grades. Here are some tips for teachers to share with parents to create an educational environment at home for the middle school student.

Reading with Young Teens

Establish a time and place each day where the family can read a book, newspaper, or magazine together and have a discussion centered around a topic of interest to everyone. Mealtime is a great time for discussion; however, this is sometimes a hectic time, and discussions can be dominated by more practical matters, so try right after dinner before everyone scatters. In the car, discussions revolving around audiobooks encourage listening comprehension skills.

Modeling Educational Behavior

Show your child that there is a purpose to reading and pursuing educational activities by engaging in them yourself. For example, have a favorite book you are reading in plain sight, encourage your child to help you find a new recipe in a magazine or cookbook, explain how to read stock prices in the newspaper while checking your stocks (make it more interesting by pointing out the stock prices of companies that your child might recognize, like McDonald's or Abercrombie & Fitch), or research a vacation to a coveted spot together on the Internet. Here, your teen will learn that participating in educational pursuits has relevance to everyday living.

Guiding Television and Movie Watching

Monitor the television programs and movies that young teens are watching. Find out about the content of the television shows and movies your teen wants to watch before making decisions about teen viewing. Limit the amount of time he or she spends watching television each day. Encourage TV shows and movies that are educational and foster interests or hobbies.

Monitoring Video Games and the Internet

Video games are addicting, and parents need to monitor their children's use of them carefully. They need to limit the amount of time their teen spends playing games and encourage wise video game choices, such as sports or mystery games. They can use video games as a treat or purposeful recreational activity. In addition to being a place to do research, the Internet is a great communication source. Teens love to come home from school and talk to their friends on the computer. Some of this socializing is necessary for their social growth. However, parents have to be mindful of the amount of time their teens spend instant messaging or chatting on the computer. Use parental controls offered through online sources, and know whom your child is talking to. Again, allow the child this time as a reward or purposeful recreational activity when homework is completed or during a scheduled break. Also, helping your child develop other interests and encouraging him or her to participate in after-school activities will leave less free time for idle chatting.

Monitoring Cell Phone Use

Cell phones are not allowed in most classrooms. Nevertheless, check your cell phone bill carefully to monitor the times and number of text messages that your teen may be sending. If there are excessive texts on your bill during school hours, you may want to make sure your teen knows that he or she should not be texting in class.

Encouraging After-School Activities

Enroll young teens in after-school activities like sports, dance, or chess, or encourage involvement in clubs or other organizations within the school, such as student council or teen theater groups. These can foster healthy interests and friendships, as well as provide structured learning activities beyond the hours of the traditional school day.

Following a Consistent Routine

Set specific times for recreation, structured activities, homework, family interaction, and bedtime. Setting schedules gives adolescents patterns and conditioning for behaviors that foster a productive home and work environment for all family members.

Setting High but Realistic Standards

Encourage and praise your teen when he or she does his or her best, whatever the outcome. Teens are sensitive to criticism. If it is constructive and realistic, it can foster growth. Asking a child to get As in science when he or she does not have the aptitude is unrealistic and can have a negative impact on his or her self-esteem and cause unnecessary hurt feelings.

Handling Homework

At this point in a child's schooling, the student should complete homework alone, with the parents ensuring that the work is being done and serving as a resource to their child. Sometimes teachers send home specific homework assignments designed to include family members. These help to stress the importance of education and show its relevance to real-life situations.

Establishing Positive Communications

At the middle school level, collaborating effectively with families is somewhat different than it is at the elementary school level. Middle school teachers are specialists and are often responsible for at least five classes and over a hundred students in their content areas. Students no longer want their parents in the classroom, as was often encouraged at the elementary school level. Collaboration with telephone calls, report cards, and progress sheets are effective methods of communication between home and school, but all too often they become the only way parents and teachers communicate. Many times a problem becomes bigger because parents were informed too late.

In an inclusive classroom, parents are often needed as volunteer participants to monitor activities and prepare and organize supplies for the students, so it becomes easier to encourage parent participation. The teacher can recruit and organize parents using a volunteer sheet, where a few parents can rotate to aid in assisting station activities on a monthly basis. This way, parents have a productive way to visit the classroom and become involved. Their help in the classroom can certainly facilitate dialogue with their child about school, and their extra hands are usually more than welcome.

Also, if a parent has a particular talent that he or she would like to share with the class that is relevant to what is being covered in the curriculum, this should be encouraged. When the seventh-grade science class is studying animals and their habitats, a parent who is a veterinarian could speak to the students about practicing veterinary medicine, for example. Teachers can also send out a monthly classroom newsletter to inform parents of the activities that will take place that month. This will keep the parents informed of exactly what is happening and will contribute to open lines of communication, making it easier to handle any problems that might develop.

Tips for Talking with Parents

Even the most experienced and enthusiastic teachers run into problems and concerns with students from time to time. When talking to a parent, make sure you employ the following techniques, and always remember that the goal is to solve the problem and promote effective learning for all students in the classroom:

- Before the meeting, make an outline of what you want to say, and role-play the meeting to yourself.
- Try to talk in person. Face-to-face encounters usually leave less room for incorrect interpretation.
- Listen first. Allow the parent to talk first. There is nothing worse than talking about your concerns, only to find out that the parent has a different agenda.
- Always talk about the student's positive attributes first. Then state the problem.
- Speak slowly, clearly, and concisely.
- State the facts of the problem.
- Paraphrase all parent questions before answering. This will foster understanding.
- Check periodically for understanding or feedback from the parent while you are talking.
- Develop a plan of action with the parent that you mutually agree on and in which you are both active participants.
- Develop a second plan of action in case the initial plan does not work.
- Decide on a designated time when you can meet again to assess progress.

Whether to have the student present at these meetings should be decided between parent and teacher individually, because everyone reacts differently to teacher meetings.

The process of teaching is exciting and challenging, and it requires strong leadership and interpersonal skills. As with all other challenges, teaching can be overwhelming, especially when children are not responding to instruction. School personnel are in place to address specific student behaviors and learning needs when they occur. Part of the art of teaching is knowing when it is appropriate to seek out specific specialized personnel.

We hope this chapter has helped you focus on how to use support services while building positive communication lines with students and their families.

Chapter 2

Preparing for Differentiated Learning

Children learn at different rates and in different ways. This chapter is designed to help you define various special needs as well as learning strengths and weaknesses. Defining and understanding students' specific learning needs will aid in successfully adapting instruction in the classroom, which will maximize all students' potential for academic success.

Working with Core Curriculum Standards

Adapting instruction to work for general and special education students begins with following the core curriculum standards for each grade being taught. These standards, designed by the U.S. Department of Education, serve as an outline for specific content objectives that must be accomplished at each grade level. Each objective includes goals stating what specific material must be covered in order for the student to attain mastery. The differentiated teaching techniques you use must be able to get across these core curriculum standards and content objectives to all students in the inclusive classroom.

Assessing Learning Styles

Identifying the learning styles of your students is important when you are planning differentiated teaching strategies. Knowing their styles allows you to group students effectively for small-group or station instruction. Student learning styles fall into three main groups: visual, auditory, and tactile or kinesthetic learners.

- *Visual learners.* Visual learners learn best by seeing information. They work well when they can copy down information in notebooks to use for studying later. Visual learners often jot things down; they are list makers and doodlers and use scrap paper for math and written expression. They like to use maps, charts, and diagrams. They are better able to listen when they have eye contact. Employing advanced organizers or planners, graphic organizers, which map information in a succinct format, review guides, and highlighting important facts are good strategies to aid visual learners.
- *Auditory learners.* Auditory learners learn best through listening. Unlike with visual learners, printed information often means little to auditory learners until the information is explained or told to them. They are strong interpreters of meaning through body language, voice inflection, tone, rhythm, and rate of a speaker. They enjoy a good lecture and usually do quite well in a large classroom setting. Reinforcement of information in the classroom for auditory learners is best done using books on tape or by tape-recording lessons. Other strategies that aid auditory learners are reading text material aloud; subvocalization or whispering instead of silent reading; studying with a tutor, family member, or friend who can discuss the information; or reciting mnemonic devices.
- *Tactile or kinesthetic learners.* These students learn best through using multisensory strategies or a hands-on approach, because they interpret information through their sense of self in space. They benefit from manipulatives, small-group assignments, role playing, building, games, moving around, and project-based learning.

Have students fill out the questionnaire on the next page to help you determine their learning styles. Check individual student responses against the Assessing Student Learning Style Answer Key below. See what learning style or styles are most prevalent in each student, and use these results for differentiated program planning. Results can also be shared at parent conferences or with students throughout the year.

Assessing Student Learning Style Answer Key

1. visual
2. visual
3. auditory
4. tactile/kinesthetic
5. auditory
6. tactile/kinesthetic
7. visual
8. visual
9. visual
10. auditory
11. tactile/kinesthetic
12. auditory
13. auditory
14. tactile/kinesthetic
15. tactile/kinesthetic

What Type of Learner Am I?

Name: _____ Date: _____

Respond with a Y (yes), N (no), or S (sometimes) to the following statements:

_____ 1. When the teacher talks, I write down everything that is said.

_____ 2. I love to make lists and cross off items when they are completed.

_____ 3. Studying with a parent or friends helps me to remember information.

_____ 4. I enjoy cooking to learn math with the class and am often put in charge to organize my group.

_____ 5. If I don't understand something, I'll read it "under my breath" to myself so only I can hear it.

_____ 6. I took first place with my science fair project two years in a row.

_____ 7. I love to read instructions and put things together.

_____ 8. I often use scrap paper before writing an essay.

_____ 9. I get upset if I leave my notes in my locker to review before a quiz.

_____ 10. I like to listen to oral presentations in class.

_____ 11. Role-playing characters and situations in literature is exciting and fun and helps me remember the story.

_____ 12. I understand information best when the teacher explains it in front of the room to the whole class.

_____ 13. I get enjoyment from listening to audiobooks.

_____ 14. I understand geometry concepts when I can build or manipulate different shapes.

_____ 15. The best review is through team games in class.

Multiple Intelligences and Learning Strengths

Howard Gardner, a professor of education at Harvard University, developed the theory of multiple intelligences. He posits that there are seven specific intelligences that individuals possess, and these intelligences, or learning strengths, can positively influence a teacher's approach to teaching styles and the learning process.

Visual/Spatial Intelligence

Students with this type of intelligence show strengths in their ability to perceive visual information. They usually think in pictures instead of words. Clues to middle school students who are visual/spatial learners are those who take copious notes; enjoy reading silently; are good map and diagram readers; and profit from handouts, study guides, or written reviews. Other clues that students have strengths in visual/spatial intelligence are that these students enjoy putting puzzles together, have a good sense of direction, enjoy building and construction tasks, and like to sketch and draw. Careers that often interest these learners include art, interior design, mechanics, architecture, and engineering.

Verbal/Linguistic Intelligence

These students love to use words and language. They learn best through listening tasks and are usually eloquent speakers. Verbal/linguistic learners usually think in words. In the classroom, these students are usually group leaders, because they formulate ideas very quickly. They enjoy listening, writing, telling stories, and even teaching the class, and they are very quick to assimilate information. At the middle school level, students who possess strengths in verbal/linguistic intelligence may be good debaters. They are also good at interpreting literature because their language skills are often strong. Career interests often include teaching, law, or writing.

Logic/Math Intelligence

Students who possess strengths in logic/math intelligence are able to reason eloquently through the use of logic and numbers. They are good problem solvers. At the middle school level, these students are often eager to participate in scientific experiments and are the first to have the answer to math word problems. They enjoy complex and abstract problems, and often understand higher-level concepts in algebra and geometry. They usually enjoy assembling models, developing science experiments, creating computer programs, and doing research projects. Professions of interest often include computer programming, engineering, science, and research.

Body/Kinesthetic Intelligence

Students with this intelligence strength are best able to express themselves through movement. These students have a good sense of the space around them and use this space to learn about their world and process information. The saying "learning by doing" applies to the way students with body/kinesthetic intelligence prefer to understand. At the middle school level, these students usually have a great sense of balance and coordination and make outstanding athletes and dancers. In the classroom, they learn best through manipulatives, building activities, role playing, and team-centered activities.

Possible careers for body/kinesthetic learners include sports, physical education, dancing, and acting.

Musical/Rhythmic Intelligence

These students learn best by thinking in sounds, rhythms, and patterns. Effective methods for these learners at the middle school level include the use of mnemonic devices and jingles to study and remember information and to identify patterns, such as in math. These learners have a strong ability to master musical and mathematical concepts. Career interests often include music composition, advertising, or mathematics.

Interpersonal Intelligence

These students have an uncanny sense of quickly seeing things from another's point of view. They are often able to predict the feelings, motivations, and intentions of others. At the middle school level, students with strong interpersonal intelligence are often class mediators. They are adept at organizing group activities and encouraging cooperation and productivity in team situations. They are naturals in using strategies for conflict resolution, communication, and encouraging positive relationships in a group. Career interests often include counseling, management, psychology, and sales.

Intrapersonal Intelligence

This type of student has strong intrapersonal skills and is often identified by peers as the voice of reason in the middle school classroom. These students are able to look at a situation objectively, understand the purpose of an activity, or interpret their roles in relationship to others. They are usually level-headed thinkers. Career interests of these learners often include psychology, psychiatry or mental health professions, or philosophy.

Fitting Teaching Strategies to Learners

It is important to realize that students have intelligence aptitude in all areas, but typically excel in two or three of the intelligence categories Gardner identified. Understanding this information and using strategies that complement individual and group strengths will help you build a classroom that is supportive, nurturing, and able to foster academic progress in all students. Page 22 will help teachers determine individual student intelligence characteristics.

Planning for Students with Special Needs

The main goal of an inclusive classroom that provides differentiated instruction at the middle school level is to provide an appropriate education for all students, covering core curriculum content, goals, and objectives relevant to the specific grade level. Students in this flexible setting will have access to high-quality science instruction and the support they need to be successful, regardless of their learning disabilities, paces, academic levels, behaviors, learning styles, or overall strengths and weaknesses. It is understood that if a student's disabilities are so severe that he or she is unable to function in this least restrictive and flexible setting, then an appropriate program placement decision would be suggested and implemented by the Child Study Team.

Identifying Intelligence Characteristics in the Middle School Classroom

Identify which type of intelligence is most likely to be associated with the description of a middle school student in the following list. Use the abbreviations in the key at the bottom of the page.

This student:

_____ 1. enjoys reading silently at his or her seat after class work is completed.

_____ 2. is a strong debater.

_____ 3. likes role-playing short stories with a group.

_____ 4. writes jingles to remember Civil War dates as a homework assignment.

_____ 5. explains the concept of longitude and latitude to other students with ease.

_____ 6. is adept at researching the answers to abstract problems for the class when asked.

_____ 7. is a good listener.

_____ 8. volunteers to paint a mural for Earth Day.

_____ 9. organizes group activities during recess.

_____ 10. is often sought out by other students for a reasonable opinion.

Abbreviations Key	Answers
V/S = visual/spatial	1. V/S
V/L = verbal/linguistic	2. V/L
L/M = logic/math	3. B/K
B/K = body/kinesthetic	4. M/R
M/R = musical/rhythmic	5. L/M
Inter = interpersonal	6. L/M
Intra = intrapersonal	7. Inter
	8. V/S
	9. Inter
	10. Intra

Teachers in an inclusive setting can expect to teach students with a multitude of abilities. They need to become skillful at adapting instruction within the classroom. Students with learning disabilities, visual and auditory impairments, ADD/ADHD, resistant learners, students with emotional and behavioral concerns, and gifted students are among the more typical types of student in an inclusive classroom setting.

Learning Disabled Students

Children with a learning disability, according to federal law, possess "a disorder involved in understanding spoken or written language, manifesting itself in an imperfect ability to think, speak, read, write, spell, or do math calculations." It is diagnosed as a severe discrepancy between their ability and their achievement in phonics, reading comprehension, mathematics, or oral and written expression. A learning disability may be neurological or perceptual. Dyslexia, minimal brain dysfunction, and aphasia are all considered learning disabilities. Learning disabilities are found on a continuum, meaning they can range from minimal to severe. Students may need adaptations to help them in school, such as extra time on a task, study guides, reteaching, or multisensory strategies in order to master class content.

Visually Impaired Students

Children who are visually impaired are considered disabled if their vision impedes their educational performance after correction. Assessments by specialists are necessary to determine if a student has a visual impairment. Students who have been identified as being visually impaired should be referred to the Commission of the Blind and Visually Impaired by the Child Study Team. The commission can offer the school information regarding specific strategies and teaching supplies useful for teaching these children. Strategies such as preferential seating, recording lectures, using large manipulatives, and writing with thick markers are just a few techniques that help to differentiate instruction for these learners.

Auditory Impaired Students

A student who has an impairment in hearing, either mild or severe, fluctuating or permanent, that has a negative impact on his or her educational performance can be diagnosed as auditory impaired. This diagnosis must be obtained through an assessment with an audiologist and speech and language specialist to determine the degree of educational impact and level of program planning. Strategies such as preferential seating, repeating and restating instructions, breaking information into simple sentences, using visual examples, and speaking slowly and clearly are just a few ways to differentiate instruction for these students. If hearing loss is moderate to severe, the use of an FM system, with which the teacher speaks directly into a small microphone attached to the small hearing device the student uses, may also be appropriate.

Physically Disabled Students

Students with physical disabilities are often aided by the development of a 504 Plan, a legal document falling under the federal Rehabilitation Act (1973), which guarantees students with medical concerns receive modifications to their programs to ensure that temporary or permanent physical disabilities do not handicap the students' educational progress in school. The medical condition or disability must be diagnosed by a physician. Students in wheelchairs, those with hemophilia, those with diabetes, and students diagnosed with central auditory processing disorders are among those with the most common medical conditions covered under 504 Plans. A 504 Plan is not considered part of special education. However, modifications to student programs, such as permanent elevator privileges, an additional set of books, preferential seating, physical education exemptions, and use of behavioral modification strategies, are often part of a student's program.

Resistant Learners and Students with Attention Deficit Disorders, With or Without Hyperactivity

A student who is resistant to learning can range from having a typical "teenage attitude" of noncompliance to a full-blown behavioral disability that compromises learning. Students with oppositional qualities, emotional disturbances, stressful home lives, anger issues, bipolar disorder, or poor impulse control can be difficult to manage in the classroom. They often require specific teaching and behavioral techniques designed to engage them in the learning process, keep them motivated, and make them feel good about themselves. Strategies for the teacher may include giving immediate and frequent forms of positive feedback, as well as using constructive criticism wisely.

Students with attention or focusing issues are often labeled by teachers as resistant learners. Often students with attention deficit disorder (ADD) or attention deficit–hyperactivity disorder (ADHD) will get off track and accomplish very little without constant redirection. Modifications include a teaching style that provides constant feedback, with tasks that are small, interactive, and presented as single concepts. For students with ADHD, a behavioral chart to monitor impulse control with tangible rewards may be an incentive to stay focused throughout the lesson.

Gifted Learners

Gifted learners present a specific set of needs to the classroom teacher and are often overlooked because they can easily accomplish what is required of them. Nevertheless, these students are often not challenged sufficiently. They can appear to be daydreamers or bored in school. Sometimes this boredom can lead to behavioral concerns. Identification of a gifted student can take place through teacher observation and recommendations; standardized test scores; report card grades; and results of diagnostic instruments, namely a test of cognitive skills. Many times a student is gifted and talented in one or two subject areas but not in others. A student can be both gifted and learning disabled at the same time. Sometimes a student is exceptional in all areas.

Strategies in the differentiated classroom for reaching gifted learners include expansion of planned lessons through small-group projects, research, problem solving, and creativity. These expansions are designed to bring the basic lesson plan to a more sophisticated and abstract level.

The inclusive classroom is designed to provide appropriate educational instruction to students with various learning styles, strengths, weaknesses, and special needs. When instruction is modified to meet their educational levels, all students can participate in one classroom, learning the same information and accomplishing very similar academic goals.

Chapter 3

Effective Teaching Strategies for Differentiating Instruction

Teaching in an inclusive classroom and differentiating instruction are not new concepts. It can be traced to the time when several grades made up one classroom, and instruction was tailored to individual student levels. Differentiating instruction may simply be the definition of effective teaching. To be effective, teachers must familiarize themselves with individual student learning levels, learning styles, strengths, weaknesses, and overall abilities in order to plan successful lessons each day. Students who need specific adaptations must also be supported with classroom staff and materials. However, teachers who invest time learning the abilities and personalities of their students will better be able to address their specific learning, behavioral, and social needs.

Tips for Effective Teaching
- Take an interest in your students.
- Establish a positive atmosphere.
- Be clear and concise when speaking.
- Be enthusiastic.
- Develop rules, and follow them.
- Do not bring personal business to the classroom.

- Make learning fun.
- Be an observer.
- Use resource professionals.
- Read background information on students to gain insight into their learning.
- Use repetition.
- Use a variety of materials and strategies to showcase learning differences.
- Incorporate various modalities and methods for all types of learners.
- Be a resource to families and students.
- Include families as part of the support system.
- Stay positive.
- Be a good listener.
- Make effective use of paraprofessionals and aides in the inclusive classroom, and include them in program planning.
- Invite parent participation where appropriate.
- Be flexible.

The Effective Inclusive Classroom

When setting up the inclusive classroom, the teacher must remember that it is a flexible environment that is constantly changing to meet the ongoing needs of the individuals and the group. The environment can vary from unit to unit depending on mastery levels. It includes methods that are student centered and reaches beyond the confines of the traditional classroom setting. Reinforcement, review, reteaching in various modalities, and enrichment are often accomplished through small-group stations led by teachers, paraprofessionals, or students. Peer teaching or tutoring can be done in pairs to further review information at a slower or more interactive pace. Stations use various manipulatives and modalities that showcase learning strengths and weaknesses. The list that follows gives some modifications, which will enable teachers to further individualize the learning environment.

Possible Adaptations for the Inclusive Classroom

- ☐ Offer preferential seating.
- ☐ Provide extra time on tasks.
- ☐ Have a student complete every other item on a homework assignment.
- ☐ Color-code items.
- ☐ Mask off sections of work that a student doesn't have to complete.
- ☐ Model problem-solving strategies.
- ☐ Role-play concepts as a review.
- ☐ Give students mnemonic devices.

- ☐ Make learning interactive.
- ☐ Provide manipulatives.
- ☐ Review, reteach, and reinforce information.
- ☐ Use a homework log signed by parents.
- ☐ Have students read aloud.
- ☐ Read directions aloud to students.
- ☐ Use graph paper to help students keep place value of numbers.
- ☐ Use behavioral charts and reward systems.
- ☐ Reward good behavior.
- ☐ Assign jobs to students to promote self-esteem.
- ☐ Develop a review sheet.
- ☐ Allow students to "whisper" while reading independently.
- ☐ Restate directions.
- ☐ Allow students to solve the first example of an assignment with the teacher.
- ☐ Reread the directions.
- ☐ Use a scribe.
- ☐ Use a computer for writing tasks.
- ☐ Use advanced organizers.
- ☐ Use graphic organizers.
- ☐ Shorten homework.

This system is not chaotic, because students expect to be doing different activities than their peers within the classroom. Therefore, issues of fairness do not come into play. It is a methodology in which teaching and learning strategies are tiered and varied in order to give all students an opportunity to be responsible for individual growth.

Station Teaching

Station teaching takes place when instruction is presented by teachers, paraprofessionals, or students in small groups to reinforce information covered in class. Each station is set up to review class lessons with various modalities, rates, or levels. In an inclusive classroom, a typical science lesson on, say, place value begins in a traditional fashion, with the subject area teacher presenting the concept information to the whole class. Then, depending on students' needs, one small group, or "station," may be designed to relearn the information using visual strategies. A second station may have paraprofessionals teaching information kinesthetically using manipulatives. A third station may include students working independently to expand the lesson, developing abstract word problems. Pairs of students may also work together for interactive learning or to review concepts at a slower pace. All instruction takes place simultaneously. In this way, a variety of learning adaptations and strategies, encompassing visual, auditory, and tactile styles, are presented and reinforced at different levels throughout the class period or block.

Classroom Climate

No matter how the classroom is structured or what information is being covered, the climate of the classroom is of utmost importance to foster an environment conducive to ongoing academic success. According to Deci and Flaster (1996), classrooms encouraging success for young teens are environments that satisfy and nurture basic human needs. The three most important basic needs of adolescents are to belong, to feel autonomous, and to feel competent.

- *To belong and feel connected to the larger group.* Teenagers are most likely to thrive in an environment in which they feel appreciated, connected, and comfortable. Take time to appropriately tell students the special value they bring to the classroom setting. Even students who have serious behavioral and emotional concerns should be recognized by teachers and peers for their positive attributes. Often, praise and compliments, if sincere, are the very components that teens are craving throughout the school day.
- *To feel autonomous.* Motivation is increased when students feel that they have some control over what is going on in their lives. They are less likely to see the worth of the learning process if they believe learning is irrelevant to their immediate world. Also, they need to have a voice in learning situations. Teenagers respond less readily to adult authority if they believe that they are being imposed on by teacher standards or that adults do not understand them.
- *To feel competent.* Teens need to feel respected for their efforts without ridicule. They need to feel that they are worthy and smart. They also need to see the intrinsic value in constructive criticism and learn to not take it personally.

Measuring Success

There are as many ways to measure success in the inclusive classroom as there are different types of students. Consider a variety of assessment techniques to evaluate each student.

Standardized Tests

Today, measuring success through test scores has become more important than ever before. The results of standardized district and state tests can weigh heavily on a student's placement and career path. With the advent of No Child Left Behind, the increasing pressure on schools to show the proficiency of teachers and programs using test score results causes much stress at all levels. Teachers are often designing lessons that teach to the test instead of using varied assessment techniques as a way to measure student mastery of information.

Formal standardized assessments, however, are necessary and can be very helpful when used correctly. Standardized tests provide information about how students test in particular content areas compared to others at their grade level locally and nationally. This kind of information can be helpful to school personnel when they are making class placement decisions and revamping curriculum.

Traditional Classroom Tests

Traditional classroom tests are an efficient and popular way to determine mastery of subject information. This type of assessment is usually teacher made and subject-area driven.

The teacher formulates a two- or three-page document using multiple choice, true-or-false, or essay questions, or some combination of these. Students take the test individually during one class period. The teacher grades the assessment and gives closure to the unit. Although these tests are effective, this testing method is overused. Because differentiated learners assimilate information in a variety of modalities, assessments must also be varied to give all students an opportunity to showcase their learning strengths.

Differentiated Assessment Strategies

These strategies allow teachers to individualize the assessment method to fit each student. Students will have varied ways of showing that they have mastered the content other than a traditional test. This results in increased success for the students.

Student-Teacher Interview

Interviews at the end of a lesson or unit can be an effective tool to check student mastery of information and learning perceptions. Individual dialogue with the teacher gives students with strong verbal abilities and intrapersonal skills a chance to talk about their strengths and weaknesses in the subject area. You can then assess knowledge and progress through discussion as well as offer constructive criticism in a nonthreatening setting.

Small-Group Presentations

Assessing how students work together in class to present information is another way to determine mastery. Observe the group as they work together to organize and give the presentation to gain insight into student participation and interpersonal skills. After the presentation, each member of the group receives an individual and a group grade.

Self-Evaluation

Students can become adept at evaluating their own work. Allow students to rate their finished products or evaluate what they have learned by answering questions, completing student surveys, or filling out checklists. You can review student answers against their own opinions and discuss the progress made. Often, students are their own best critics.

Demonstrations and Oral Reports

This type of evaluation is advantageous for visual/linguistic, auditory, and kinesthetic learners. Here, students assimilate information and communicate, or "teach," information to the rest of the class. Because these learners are adept with vocabulary skills, it is a great way for the classroom teacher to assess concept accuracy.

Project-Centered Evaluation

Science and math lend themselves well to this type of evaluation. Students create a project, such as a poster or dramatic presentation, that brings together the concepts they learned during the unit. Students with visual/spatial and logic/math intelligence usually exhibit strengths when this type of assessment is used as an evaluation tool. Use previously stated or agreed-on criteria with the class when using this assessment method.

An inclusive classroom allows all students equal access to the same standards as well as equal opportunities to illustrate their understanding of the concepts. You can achieve this through your instructional methods as well as using varied assessment techniques. The end result will be a group of students with improved scientific confidence as they experience success.

Part Two

Science Activities for the Inclusive Middle School Classroom

Chapter 4

Scientific Inquiry

Activity 1: Scientific Method

Purpose: This activity will help students understand the method by which scientists approach problems and solutions.

Read through the lesson and the adaptations and make sure you have the supplies you will need.

Supplies for the main lesson

chalkboard, overhead projector, computer with presentation software, or interactive whiteboard

science notebooks

Supplies for the adaptations

flip chart

colored markers

colored construction paper for the graphic organizer

Lesson

1. Begin by saying something like, "Today we are going to talk about the scientific method. When scientists approach problems and look for solutions, they use a systematic approach. Like most successful problem solvers, they combine this with imagination, prior knowledge, and persistence. This could involve observation, collection of data, and putting together pieces of information in order to draw conclusions or make hypotheses. Using the scientific method is a typical way a scientist may approach a problem to find a solution."

2. Write the following notes on the board for students to copy down in their notebooks:

Scientific Method

    a. State the problem.

    b. Gather information.

    c. Develop a hypothesis. (A hypothesis is an interpretation of the information gathered by the scientist.)

    d. Perform experiments to test the accuracy of the hypothesis.

    e. Record and analyze the data collected.

    f. State a conclusion.

3. Now say, "Let's pose an everyday problem and attempt to solve it using this scientific method." Include students in this brainstorming exercise during each step:

    a. State the problem: "The DVD player doesn't work; we can't watch the movie we rented."

b. Gather information about what you know might have gone wrong regarding a DVD player:

- Is the chord plugged in?
- Is the DVD player turned on?
- Is the TV screen or monitor turned on?
- Is the light for the cable lit?
- Is the cable at the back of the DVD player sufficiently connected to the machine?
- Is anything stuck in the player?
- Was there a power outage?

c. Develop a hypothesis: It is possible that we cannot watch the movie because one of the above points is causing the player not to work.

d. Perform experiments to check the hypothesis: Check to make sure all of the components identified in the information-gathering stage are in working order.

e. Record and analyze your data: Analyze the experiments performed and data collected. Did any of these points solve the problem?

f. State a conclusion: Depending on what you found and adjusted, try playing the movie again. If it works, the problem has been solved in a systematic fashion. If not, some more data collection and analysis may be needed.

Explain that scientists use this same type of thought process to analyze problems and develop scientific solutions.

Hand out the Scientific Method Worksheet and proceed to work with small groups of students on some of the adaptations. Also, if time permits, have the students participate in the Whole Class Lab at the end of this activity.

Name: _____ Date: _____

Scientific Method Worksheet

Pick one of the following situations and use the scientific method to systematically find solutions to the problem.

    Your cell phone will not give you a signal.

    Your dogs bark every night at 11:00 PM.

    Cookies made from a favorite recipe burn every time you make them.

    Your skateboard wheels will not turn.

1. State the problem.

    _____

    _____

2. Gather information on the problem.

    _____

    _____

    _____

3. Develop a hypothesis.

    _____

    _____

    _____

4. Test your hypothesis.

    _____

    _____

    _____

5. Record and analyze the data.

    _____

    _____

    _____

6. State a conclusion.

    _____

    _____

    _____

How to Adapt This Lesson for the Inclusive Classroom

For Learning Disabled Students

For students who struggle to remember and understand the steps in this scientific method, the following mnemonic can be used to streamline the concepts taught in class:

The SCIENCE Strategy

S = State the problem.

CI = Collect Information.

E = Experiment with data.

N = Note and record the results.

C = Contemplate solutions.

E = Evaluate and state a conclusion.

Place this strategy on a flip chart so students can see it while they are working. Review and reteach using this strategy before having students begin the worksheet. Also, if worksheet problems seem too difficult, you can brainstorm with students to choose a more familiar topic than the one presented.

For Students with Visual or Cognitive Difficulties

Use construction paper to make a graphic organizer. A graphic organizer is a visual representation of chunks of information. Have students answer "W" questions, such as who, what, when, where, or why, about the problem and solutions. The visual representation may help students to more accurately grasp how the scientific method is used.

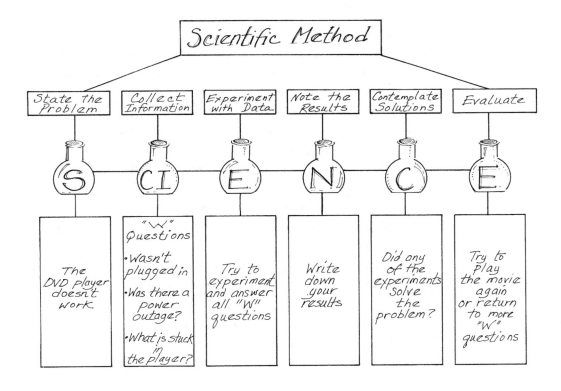

For Students with Behavioral Difficulties or ADD/ADHD

Allow each student who understands the process to individually tutor a student who needs help completing the graphic organizer. Putting these students in charge of aiding others in completing an assignment will be empowering and interactive, and will serve as a focusing tool.

For Gifted Learners

Expand on this lesson by having students research a famous invention or scientific discovery and hypothesize about how the scientist may have used the scientific method to explain results and draw conclusions. Students may work in the media center and consult with the media specialist or use a search engine on the computer to research scholarly or scientific articles. Have them record the information they gather and read this to the class.

Whole Class Lab: Making "Funny Putty"

Purpose: This fun, hands-on activity requires students to use the scientific method. This lab works best with groups of three or four students.

Supplies (per group)

¼ cup of white glue

¼ cup of liquid starch

4 drops of food coloring

small bowl

wooden spoon

¼ measuring cup

1. Have students place glue and starch in their small bowls.
2. They then mix gently with wooden spoons. Students should run the wooden spoons under warm water as soon as they are done stirring so that glue does not ruin them.
3. Have students add food coloring to their mixtures and then take turns kneading the dough with their hands until the consistency changes.
4. Then have students answer the following questions on lined paper with their groups using the principals of the scientific method, before handing in their completed labs.

   a. What were you attempting to make?

   b. What ingredients were collected and combined? What happened after stirring the starch and glue together?

   c. What did you think would happen once you added the food coloring? Once you began kneading? What actually happened?

   d. How long did you think it would take before the substance changed its consistency? How long did it actually take?

   e. What was the end result of this experiment? What can you conclude about mixing these ingredients?

How to Adapt This Lab for the Inclusive Classroom

For Students with Fine Motor or Perceptual Difficulties

Allow these students to complete less complex fine motor tasks, such as mixing and kneading, instead of measuring ingredients.

For Students with Behavioral Difficulties or ADD/ADHD

Empower these students and pique their interests by placing them in charge of the lab reports and the managing of lab tasks.

Home/School Connection

Give students the following assignment to complete at home:

> Search online or in a newspaper or magazine for an article on a scientific discovery. Copy or cut it out and discuss it with your family members. Write a one-page essay hypothesizing how scientists may have used the scientific method to draw the conclusions found in the article. Bring the article and your essay to class for further discussion.

How to Evaluate This Lesson

We suggest a small-group assignment as a means of assessment for this activity. Have students assemble into groups of four students. Write the following on the whiteboard:

Problem: The local reservoirs are dangerously low this year.

Ask students to brainstorm this problem and use the scientific method to come up with feasible ways to conserve water during this shortage. Students can then write down their findings, explanations, and conclusions and hand them in for a group grade.

Activity 2: Famous Scientists

Purpose: This activity aims to inspire students by exposing them to famous scientists and their contributions to society.

Read through the lesson and the adaptations and make sure you have the supplies you will need.

Supplies for the main lesson

chalkboard, overhead projector, computer with presentation software, or interactive whiteboard

science notebooks

Supplies for the adaptations

highlighters

notecards

computer version of worksheet

Lesson

1. Begin by saying something like, "Today we are going to learn about and explore the works of many historical and contemporary scientists. We will examine how these works have benefited the society we live in today."

2. Brainstorm with the class, leading students to various advancements in medicine and technology, and formulate a list on the board. Such developments as penicillin, antibiotics, vaccines, computers, cell phones, chemotherapy, and so on can be included on this list. Students should copy the list into their notebooks.

If students struggle with the concept of scientific advancement, tell them to close their eyes and visualize the start of the day. Have them think about, for example, turning on the lights, making coffee, listening to the radio, checking cell phone messages, taking vitamins, taking a shower, and so on. Remind them that all of these events involve scientific discoveries that have had an impact on our lives.

3. Now say, "Let's research and formulate a list of scientists, scientific discoveries, and the impact of these developments on society today." Pass out lined paper divided into four columns, or pass out a premade table (see next page).

4. Fill out the Scientist and Scientific Discovery parts of the list with the students in class. Then take the students to the computer lab to research and fill out the rest of the information in their tables independently.

5. Assign each student a scientist from the list to research further.

Hand out the Famous Scientists Worksheet and proceed to work with small groups of students on some of the adaptations. Also, if time permits, have the students participate in the Whole Class Lab at the end of this activity.

Scientist	Scientific Discovery	Year(s) of Discovery	Impact on Society

Name: _____   Date: _____

Famous Scientists Worksheet

Fill in the blanks in the questions that follow.

Name of scientist: _____

Date of birth: _____

Contribution to the field of science: _____

Year of contribution, invention, or discovery: _____

Briefly explain the contribution, invention, or discovery.

_____

_____

_____

_____

_____

_____

What positive changes occurred in society as a result of this contribution, invention, or discovery? Explain in detail.

_____

_____

_____

_____

_____

_____

_____

_____

How to Adapt This Lesson for the Inclusive Classroom

For Learning Disabled Students

Allow the students to make copies of the research found in books, magazines, or on the Internet. Assist students in highlighting the information needed to complete the worksheet.

For Delayed Readers

Assist the students in finding video or audio materials to use in their research. After they have completed their research, students can read aloud and highlight the information needed regarding their scientific discoveries. Assist students with highlighting and defining key scientific terms. Write words phonetically on note cards to aid in pronunciations.

Allow students to reread the highlighted information for additional comprehension. Create a dialogue with the students, asking them to visualize what the information means. Have them recreate sentences in their own words. Coach the students to sequence the information and fill out their worksheets.

For Students with Fine Motor or Perceptual Difficulties

Make a computerized version of the worksheet. Allow students to use computer skills to copy and paste information found during their computer searches directly into the document. Assist students in retyping this information in their own words. They can then print out the finished worksheet to hand in. This will minimize the need for transferring and writing skills.

For Gifted Learners

Allow students to create a PowerPoint presentation about their scientists and present to the class.

Whole Class Lab: Scientific Contributions

Purpose: This lab is designed to increase students' exposure to and knowledge of historical and contemporary scientific discoveries, inventions, or contributions in society.

It works best if completed by small groups of students in three one-hour time blocks.

Supplies

note cards listing various contemporary and historical scientists not yet covered in class

1. Each group will pick a scientist from the deck of cards.

2. Groups will research their chosen scientists, determining their contributions, histories, and time lines.

3. Then have each group create a skit that explains how the scientist improved society and how we benefit from his or her contribution today. Encourage students to use props, and give all lab groups time to practice their skits.

4. Each group will present their skit while the other students make a list of the scientists and their contributions.

How to Adapt This Lab for the Inclusive Classroom

For Resistant Learners or Students with Behavioral Difficulties

The student who feels very self-conscious speaking in front of the class may contribute to his or her group by being a narrator, collecting props, writing dialogue, researching, or managing the skit production.

Home/School Connection

Give students the following assignment to complete at home (allow about three weeks for students to complete this activity):

> With the help of your family, create your own mini-invention and make a drawing or a three-dimensional model of it to bring to class. Come to class prepared to discuss how you used the scientific method to create your invention, how it works, and how it would benefit society.

How to Evaluate This Lesson

Evaluate this unit based on the Home/School Connection oral presentation explaining the purpose of the student's invention, how it would work, and how it would benefit society.

Chapter 5

Physical Science

Activity 1: Force

Purpose: Students will come to understand the laws of force and apply them to real-life situations.

Read through the lesson and the adaptations and make sure you have the supplies you will need.

Supplies for the main lesson

chalkboard, overhead projector, computer with presentation software, or interactive whiteboard

science notebooks

Supplies for the adaptations

construction paper

scissors

assorted colored markers

note cards

computer paper

Lesson

1. Begin by saying something like, "Today we are going to define and explore the concept of force in science. The formal definition of force is the pushing or pulling on an object. An example of a force pushing is the act of blowing out candles. An example of a force pulling is the attraction of a magnet. All forces give energy to objects. Some forces interfere with motion. Two examples of this are friction and gravity."

2. Define friction and gravity and write the definitions on the board. Have the students copy the following definitions down in their notebooks:

   a. **Friction:** Friction is a force that brings an object to rest. It opposes the pushing or pulling energy and slows it down. There are three main types of friction.

   Slide Friction: Slide friction occurs when two surfaces glide or slide over each other. An example of this involves ice skating. The skates' blades travel across the ice, but the two surfaces' meeting each other actually slows the skater down.

   Rolling Friction: Rolling friction is similar to slide friction. An example of rolling friction involves the wheels on a car or bicycle. The wheels are needed to make the object move smoothly, yet it is the contact between the two surfaces that controls the motion that is created.

   Fluid Friction: Fluid friction occurs when air, water, or oil cause resistance between two forces. An example of fluid friction involves an eagle soaring in flight. The wings' meeting the air generates fluid friction and resistance. This controls the speed of the eagle's flight.

b. **Gravity:** Gravity is the natural force between objects and the earth. Gravity acts as a natural resistance, pulling all objects to the earth at the same rate.

3. Then explain balanced and unbalanced forces, saying, "Forces between objects can be balanced or unbalanced. If forces are equal yet opposite, they are considered balanced, and no change in motion occurs. A backpack sitting on top of a desk is an example of a balanced force. Gravity pushes the backpack down, and the force of the desk holds it up. The forces are equal, so no motion occurs. An unbalanced force, however, always contains motion. Two children on a seesaw, for example, represent an unbalanced force when one child is heavier than the other."

Hand out the Force Worksheet and proceed to work with small groups of students on some of the adaptations. Also, if time permits, have the students participate in the Whole Class Lab at the end of this activity.

Name: _____   Date: _____

Force Worksheet

Circle the best answer for each item.

1. Force can best be explained as:
   a. motion and resistance
   b. rolling friction
   c. the moving of an object
   d. the pushing and pulling of an object

2. A force that slows down motion is:
   a. inertia
   b. acceleration
   c. friction
   d. none of the above

3. An example of sliding friction involves:
   a. a cart rolling down a hill
   b. a skater gliding on ice
   c. diving in a pool
   d. a tug of war

4. Swimming laps in a pool is an example of:
   a. unbalanced forces
   b. inertia
   c. sliding friction
   d. fluid friction

5. An arm wrestling match in which one person is winning is best described as having:
   a. unbalanced forces
   b. sliding friction
   c. gravity
   d. fluid friction

6. A parked car is best described as having:
   a. gravitational force
   b. acceleration
   c. balanced forces
   d. rolling friction

7. The force of attraction between objects and the earth is called:
   a. gravity
   b. friction
   c. energy
   d. motion

8. Fluid friction is best explained by:
   a. a skateboarder learning a skateboard trick
   b. a hot air balloon landing in a field
   c. a book sitting on a table
   d. a child riding a bicycle

How to Adapt This Lesson for the Inclusive Classroom

For Learning Disabled Students

Students can record notes in a graphic organizer or on a partial notes form, as shown. Partial notes are notes started by the teacher and completed by the students. The extra content information provided helps the student stay organized and remain on task.

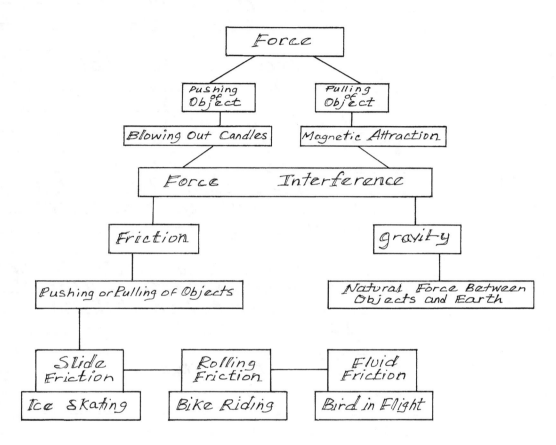

Rephrase and restate the notes to ensure student understanding. Students can also cover up the answer choices on the worksheet, first answering using the self-talk strategy. Using a self-talk strategy helps students to hear, understand, and organize the metacognitive steps needed to solve problems. For example, the student will say aloud, "First I will read the question, then I will say the answer, then I will write the answer." They can then look for their answers among the choices.

For Students with Cognitive Difficulties

Reteach the concepts relating to force, drawing and color coding simple pictures on note cards to illustrate meanings. Or have students make their own cards. Students should keep the cards visible as a memory and learning aid while completing their worksheets.

For Delayed Readers

Read each item on the worksheet aloud to the students. For each question, ask them to reread the question, close their eyes, and visualize what the question is asking. Have

> *Force*
> a) *Pushing of an object - Ex.* ——————
> b) *Pulling of an object - Ex.* ——————
>
> *Force Interference*
> a) *Friction –*
>
> b) *gravity –*
>
> *Types of Friction*
> a) *Slide Friction – This occurs when two surfaces glide over each other. Ex.* ——————
>
> b) *Rolling Friction – This occurs when contact between two surfaces controls the motion that is created. Ex.* ——————
>
> c) *Fluid Friction –*
>
> *Ex.* ——————

students cover all but one of the answer choices on their worksheets with a strip of construction paper. Then read the question and ask students to think about only the uncovered choice to decide if this answer is correct or not. If not, they should cross the item off their worksheets and proceed until they arrive at the correct answer.

For Gifted Learners

Have students design and make paper airplanes. Tell students to build a plane that will travel as far as possible, taking into account friction, gravity, and force, as covered in class. They should then write a one-page essay both explaining how they constructed their planes and documenting their flying outcomes.

Whole Class Lab: Tug of War

Purpose: This lab is designed to illustrate balanced and unbalanced forces.

It works best with the whole class outside or in the gym. Students should all be wearing sneakers.

Supplies

rope

paper

pencils

stopwatch, analog watch with a second hand, or digital watch with seconds

1. Choose two fairly equal teams.
2. Have each team take an end of the rope.
3. Begin timing and have the two teams start to pull. Have a paraprofessional stand on the sidelines and mark the midpoint of the field. Record which side wins. Have students change sides and record what changes.
4. Have the students write down and hand in the answers to the following questions:
   a. What type of force was present when neither team was winning the tug of war?
   b. What happened when the first team won? When the teams were switched?
   c. What else affected the results of this activity?

How to Adapt This Lab for the Inclusive Classroom

For Students with Physical Disabilities

Students who are wheelchair bound can work with the paraprofessional to mark the midpoint of the field, serve as a referee to both teams, and record what happens during each tug of war round.

Home/School Connection

Give students the following assignment to complete at home:

> Discuss with your family several examples of fluid, sliding, and rolling friction found in your home. Write your findings on a note card and bring it to class to discuss.

How to Evaluate This Lesson

We recommend a traditional assessment for this activity. Give students each a piece of paper and ask them to define and provide one example for each of the following terms:

Rolling Friction

Sliding Friction

Balanced Forces

Unbalanced Forces

Fluid Friction

Activity 2: Motion

Purpose: This activity will teach students about Newton's Laws and how these relate to everyday living.

Read through the lesson and the adaptations and make sure you have the supplies you will need.

Supplies for the main lesson

chalkboard, overhead projector, computer with presentation software, or interactive whiteboard

science notebooks

Supplies for the adaptations

Pictures from magazines illustrating Newton's Laws (at least ten)

Lesson

1. Begin by saying something like, "Today we are going to talk about a very famous scientist named Sir Isaac Newton. Sir Isaac Newton was a physical scientist during the seventeenth century. He described three famous laws of physics that we now call Newton's Laws."

2. Write the following three laws and their definitions on the board and have students copy them down in their notebooks:

   a. **Newton's First Law:** An object at rest stays at rest; an object in motion stays in motion unless an unbalanced force acts upon it.

   b. **Newton's Second Law:** Force equals mass times acceleration.

   c. **Newton's Third Law:** For every action, there is an equal and opposite reaction.

2. Explain that you are going to explore each of Newton's Laws in depth.

3. Start with Newton's First Law, saying, "Newton's First Law can be demonstrated in a vacuum, a region where gravity is unable to interact with objects. When an object is placed in the vacuum, it stays put. Once set in motion, the object continues moving until it is manually stopped by an outside force. Picture astronauts in space, where no gravity is present. The same principal applies. Objects that are placed without movement will suspend in zero gravity and stay put, whereas objects that are placed in motion will continue moving and floating around the space. This is one reason that astronauts eat very differently in space than they would here on earth. Their food and utensils may float all around their space shuttle cabin!"

4. Next explain Newton's Second Law, saying, "Newton's second law states that the higher the mass of an object, the greater the force required to accelerate or move the object. The smaller the mass, the smaller the force required. The force applied to a body produces a proportional acceleration. If you think of automobiles, a smaller, lighter car requires less force to accelerate or move it.

A heavier car requires more force to move the car the same distance. Therefore, the smaller car requires less fuel to travel the same distance as the heavier car." Then write the following problems on the board:

F (force) = m (mass) × a (acceleration)

Say, "Let's look at the force required to move a car with a mass of 800 kilograms versus a car with a mass of 1,200 kilograms by using the above equation."

F = 800 kilograms (kg) × 3 miles per second

F = 2,400 Newtons (N)

F = 1,200 kg × 3 miles per second

F = 3,600 N (an increase of 1,200 N), which illustrates that more force is needed to accelerate a heavier car

5. Now explain Newton's Third Law, saying, "Newton's third law states that every force has an equal or opposing force. For instance, think of a bouncing ball. To bounce the ball, you push it downward to the floor. The amount of force you put on the ball is directly related to the distance the ball bounces back to you."

Hand out the Motion Worksheet and proceed to work with small groups of students on some of the adaptations. Also, if time permits, have the students participate in the Whole Class Lab at the end of this activity.

Motion Worksheet

Give a real-life example of each of Newton's Laws. Write your answers in complete sentences. You may use the Internet and class notes to find examples.

1. Newton's First Law: An object in motion stays in motion. An object at rest stays at rest unless an unbalanced force acts upon it.

   _____

   _____

   _____

   _____

   _____

   _____

2. Newton's Second Law: Force equals mass times acceleration.

   _____

   _____

   _____

   _____

   _____

   _____

3. Newton's Third Law: For every action, there is an equal and opposite reaction.

   _____

   _____

   _____

   _____

   _____

   _____

How to Adapt This Lesson for the Inclusive Classroom

For Learning Disabled Students

Play the Locomotion Game. Look in magazines, in newspapers, and online to find at least ten pictures that illustrate all three of Newton's Laws. Cut out or copy these pictures and mount and glue them on manila folders.

The Locomotion Game

1. With a marker, write each of Newton's Laws in three separate columns on the board.

2. Have students form two teams, A and B. Each team forms a line.

3. Give Team A one of the pictures. They need to decide which of Newton's Laws is shown in the picture. The first team member in the line puts the picture underneath the corresponding law on the board.

4. Team A then explains why they chose that law. If correct, Team A receives a point. If not, Team B gets a chance to find the correct law that describes the picture.

5. Give Team B the next picture and continue as above.

6. The team with the most points wins the game.

For Students with Cognitive Difficulties

Students with cognitive disabilities may also benefit from playing the Locomotion Game. If this is still too difficult, present the pictures and have students identify the laws at a slower pace, without the pressure of a game-like situation.

For Students with Fine Motor or Perceptual Difficulties

Because a large amount of writing is required for the Motion Worksheet, students struggling with fine motor or visual difficulties may draw and label pictures instead of using sentences. Allow students to use a keyboard with a larger font or enlist the help of a scribe to write examples of Newton's Laws.

For Gifted Learners

Expand on this lesson by having students research some vintage games that use Newton's Laws and principles (such as Mouse Trap, dominos, pool, or pinball). If possible, have these students bring in at least one of these games to class, demonstrate how to play the game, and describe how Newton's Laws are illustrated therein.

Whole Class Lab: A Day at the Races

This lab shows Newton's Laws in action.

It works best with small groups of four students each taking turns using the small cars and ramp.

Supplies

four small toy cars

piece of plastic track at least 6 feet long

ten 4-inch paper cups

assorted coins (pennies, nickels, and quarters)

masking tape

cardboard box, approximately 9 by 12 inches (such as a box for holding paper)

book

note cards

Side View

Top View

Car   *Coins*

1. With the help of the teacher or paraprofessional, students make a ramp by securing the plastic track to the box with masking tape. Tape the other end of the track to the floor.

2. Set paper cups at the bottom of the ramp, directly in front of the track, in a triangle formation, with four cups making up the bottom row, followed successively by three cups, two cups, and one cup.

3. Students each pick a toy car, in turn placing their cars at the top of the ramp, allowing them to roll down and crash into the cups. Have students measure the distance between the track's end and the furthest cup for each of their individual trials, recording the distances on note cards. Students can reset the cups after each trial.

4. Students should alter the motion by putting a book on top of the box to lift the top of the ramp higher and repeating the experiment, again recording the distance between the track's end and the furthest cup.

5. Students may also alter the force by taping a penny, a nickel, and a quarter to the bottom of each of their cars and repeating the experiment. They then record their results.

6. Ask students to write and submit a one-page summary of how these experiments illustrate all three of Newton's Laws.

How to Adapt This Lab for the Inclusive Classroom

For Students with Fine Motor Difficulties

Allow students to place cars on the ramp, tear tape to attach the coins to the cars, and collect cups after impact, because these tasks require a relatively low degree of fine motor control.

For Students with Physical Disabilities

The student who is wheelchair bound and has difficulties getting close to the floor can alter the motion of the car by placing the track ramp such that he or she can hold it from his or her wheelchair.

Home/School Connection

Give students the following assignment to complete at home:

> Design a game with your family that uses at least one of Newton's Laws. Bring the game to class, teach the class how to play the game, and describe how the law applies.

How to Evaluate This Lesson

We suggest an informal assessment to determine students' understanding of this lesson. Use the students' game presentations, lab results, class participation, and worksheets to determine their mastery of this concept. You may want to use the following rubric:

Game presentation	30 percent
Lab essay	35 percent
Lab and class participation	15 percent
Worksheet	20 percent

Activity 3: Properties of Matter

Purpose: Through this activity, students will determine the various types and characteristics of matter.

Read through the lesson and the adaptations and make sure you have the supplies you will need.

Supplies for the main lesson

chalkboard, overhead projector, computer with presentation software, or interactive whiteboard

science notebooks

egg

1-liter beaker

two identical shoe boxes, one empty and one with a brick or other weight inside

Supplies for the adaptations

calculator

gram scale

assorted coins

lined paper

Lesson

1. Begin by saying something like, "Today we will begin a discussion on matter. Matter can take several forms. It can be in the form of a solid, liquid, or gas. Characteristics or properties of matter can be very general or specific. General properties, such as mass, weight, volume, and density, are some useful ways to define matter. More specific properties, such as color, taste, odor, texture, shape, hardness, softness, and flexibility, serve as ways to define the uniqueness of each substance."

2. Next say, "Let's look further at the general properties of matter. We said before that general properties include mass, weight, volume, and density." Write the following definitions on the board and have students copy them down in their notebooks. Students may condense the notes by writing down the first sentence of each definition.

   a. **Mass:** Mass is the amount of matter in an object. It is a constant unless the matter itself is altered. In the case of a backpack without contents, whether the backpack is on a chair, in a desk, or in a locker it has the same mass. Only when something is put into or taken out of the backpack, such as a book, does the mass change. Mass is measured in grams (g).

   b. **Weight:** Weight is affected by mass, but it is also variable depending on gravity. The greater the mass of an object, the greater its pull to the earth, or gravitational force. However, gravitational forces, and therefore weight, may change. For example, Earth has a larger mass than the moon, so its pull on an object is greater than the moon's pull on that same object. Therefore, you would weigh much less on the moon.

c. **Volume:** Volume describes the amount of space occupied by a mass. It is measured in liters.

Matter has mass and occupies space. Therefore, matter has mass and volume.

To demonstrate how to calculate volume, fill the liter beaker ½ full of water and write down the amount. Place the egg at the bottom of the beaker and observe as a class how high the water level rises. The difference between the original measurement and the amount of water after the egg is added is the approximate volume of the egg.

d. **Density:** Density is the amount of mass per unit volume of an object. Unit volume is a standard measurement.

To demonstrate different densities, show students the shoe boxes you prepared beforehand. Have a student volunteer pick up each shoe box and determine which one has greater density. Explain that the two boxes have the same volume, but different masses, so they have different densities. Then demonstrate, explain, and write the following formulas on the board:

Density = weight ÷ volume

To find the mass of an object when given the density, the density must be multiplied by the volume:

Mass = density × volume

For example, the density of iron is 7.9 grams (g) per centimeters cubed (cm^3). If the volume of a piece of iron is 4 cm^3, then the mass of the piece of iron is 7.9 g/cm^3 × 4 cm^3, or 31.6 g.

Hand out the Properties of Matter Worksheet and proceed to work with small groups of students on some of the adaptations. Also, if time permits, have the students participate in the Whole Class Lab at the end of this activity.

Name: _____   Date: _____

Properties of Matter Worksheet

Explain the following terms in your own words. Use your notes from class as a reference.

1. Mass: _____
   _____
   _____

2. Weight: _____
   _____
   _____

3. Volume: _____
   _____
   _____

4. Density: _____
   _____
   _____

5. The formula for calculating the density of an object is:
   _____
   _____

6. If you know the volume and density of an object, what is the formula for calculating the mass?
   _____
   _____

7. If a piece of granite has a mass of 27 g and a volume of 10 cm^3, what is the density of the rock?
   _____
   _____

8. A piece of gold jewelry has a mass of 15 g and a volume of 2.5 cm^3. What is the density of the jewelry piece?
   _____
   _____

9. The density of a beautiful sapphire stone is 3 g/cm^3. Its volume is only 0.2 cm^3. What is the mass of the stone?
   _____
   _____

How to Adapt This Lesson for the Inclusive Classroom

For Learning Disabled Students

Review concepts regarding properties of matter using class notes. Discuss several other examples in a small group to solidify students' understanding, and write these new examples on a flip chart. Review math concepts separately, using formulas but multiplying and dividing with single-digit whole numbers. Once students have mastered these problems, proceed first to the numbers used in the lesson and then to the worksheet. Students may also use calculators to do the computations if needed.

For Students with Cognitive Difficulties

Use concrete examples to illustrate matter, weight, volume, and density, such as by comparing the contents of students' lunch bags and backpacks, or using measuring cups and gram scales to show the weight and mass of crayons, erasers, and so on. Review the notes, tie the terms into tangible examples, and discuss. Help students develop simple definitions for their worksheets.

For Students with Fine Motor or Perceptual Difficulties

Pass out graphing paper or lined paper turned horizontally, on which students can solve math equations. Students may also take notes using a graphic organizer.

For Gifted Learners

Expand on this lesson by having students use class notes, references, and equipment to determine the mass, density, volume, and weight of various coins (such as a penny, dime, nickel, quarter, and half dollar). Once they have completed their calculations, students may make a chart depicting these values and hang it up in the classroom.

Whole Class Lab: Make a Liquid Layer Cake

Purpose: In this lab, students will determine whether a given liquid is more or less dense than water.

This lab works best with groups of three or four students.

Supplies (per group)

48-ounce, clean glass jar and lid with the label removed

measuring cup equivalent to at least 240 milliliters (ml), or 1 cup size

water

food coloring

1 cup or 240 ml of olive oil

1 cup or 240 ml of pancake syrup

1 cup or 240 ml of white vinegar

1 cup or 240 ml of dishwashing detergent

note cards

computer paper

scissors

markers

tape

1. Have each group of students predict which of the sample liquids—olive oil, pancake syrup, white vinegar, and dishwashing detergent—are more or less dense than water. Liquids that have a greater density than water will sink when placed in water, and the water will float to the top. Liquids that have a lower density than water will float on top of the water. Each group should predict how their "liquid layer cake" will "stack up." When stacked, the liquids will form layers, resembling the layers of a cake.

2. Each group should begin making the cakes by measuring 240 ml of water and pouring it into their jars. They should tint the water with 4 drops of food coloring with the colors of their choice.

3. Have each group rinse out the measuring cup each time and add ¼ to ½ of a cup of the listed liquids one at a time to the jar, observing what happens. Students should determine which liquids sink and which float, seeing whether their predictions match the outcome of their liquid layer cakes.

4. Ask students to make labels for each layer and tape them on the front of the jars, hand in their predictions, and write and hand in one-page essays explaining the densities of these liquids in relation to that of water. Display the finished liquid layer cakes in the classroom.

How to Adapt This Lab for the Inclusive Classroom

For Students with Physical Disabilities or Fine Motor Difficulties

For the wheelchair-bound student, place a cutting board across the wheelchair to give an ample work surface for the student. Also, these students may need physical support and assistance when pouring and measuring liquids.

For Students with Behavioral Difficulties or ADD/ADHD

Place these students in a group of supportive students in which assistance can be given and distractions minimized.

Home/School Connection

Give students the following assignment to complete at home:

Explain mass, volume, weight, and density to a family member by filling up a sink and comparing what sinks and what floats. Use at least four items. Examples of items to compare include:

• a raw egg and a cooked egg

• a wooden spoon and a stainless steel spoon

• a can of regular soda and a can of diet soda

Make a chart of your findings and bring it to class.

How to Evaluate This Lesson

We recommend an interview format to evaluate this lesson. Talk to students individually and ask them to explain the four general properties of matter in their own words. Discuss with them the purpose of the lab, asking them what they learned by making the liquid layer cake.

Activity 4: Phases of Matter

Purpose: This activity will show students that matter can change into many forms, but the original substance remains constant.

Read through the lesson and the adaptations and make sure you have the supplies you will need.

Supplies for the main lesson

chalkboard, overhead projector, computer with presentation software, or interactive whiteboard

science notebooks

Supplies for the adaptations

blank note cards

colored pencils

markers

Lesson

1. Begin by saying something like, "Today we are going to study the three phases of matter: solid, liquid, and gas. Before we discuss this, let's talk about the meaning of the word 'phase.' If your parents say that you must be going through a 'phase,' what does that mean?"

   "A phase means a change to something that otherwise stays the same. So, when you are going through a phase, you are changing just one aspect of your behavior. When we look at the phases of matter, the definitions are not that different from when we talk about ourselves."

2. Define the three phases of matter. Write the following definitions on the board and have students copy them down in their notebooks:

   a. **Solid:** A solid has a definite shape and volume. A pen, a CD, a computer, and an ice cube are all solids. There are also two different types of solids: crystalline and amorphous.

      Crystalline Solid: A crystalline solid is made up of crystals and is hard. An example is table salt. Crystals are substances made of atoms that form a three-dimensional pattern.

      Amorphous Solid: An amorphous solid is normally solid, but loses its shape under certain conditions. An example of this is candle wax, which turns to a liquid when burned.

   b. **Liquid:** A liquid can be poured and has no definite shape. It takes on the shape of whatever contains it. A liquid does, however, have a definite volume.

   c. **Gas:** A gas does not have a definite shape or volume. Gas expands to fill its container. A gas might fill a balloon, a room, or the atmosphere.

3. Explain that phases of matter change through transitions. Changes in phase often occur when thermal energy is either absorbed or released. Have students take notes on the possible transitions and write them in their notebooks.

a. **Solid → Liquid:** For a solid to change to a liquid, melting has to occur. The point at which the solid changes to a liquid is called its melting point.

b. **Liquid → Solid:** A liquid can change into a solid by freezing. The point at which a liquid turns into a solid is called its freezing point.

c. **Liquid → Gas:** Liquids change into gas through vaporization. Vaporization occurs when a liquid reaches its boiling point. A liquid can turn to vapor below its boiling point through the process of evaporation.

d. **Gas → Liquid:** A gas can turn into a liquid through condensation.

e. **Gas → Solid:** The process in which a gas turns into a solid is called deposition. An example of deposition involves snow, which forms directly from water vapor without first going through the liquid phase.

f. **Solid → Gas:** Solids can turn directly into gas in a process known as sublimation. An example involves "dry ice." Normally, ice goes from a solid to a liquid state before it evaporates. But dry ice, which is made up of carbon dioxide (CO_2), cannot exist in a liquid form, so it changes from solid directly to gas.

Hand out the Phases of Matter Worksheet and proceed to work with small groups of students on some of the adaptations. Also, if time permits, have the students participate in the Whole Class Lab at the end of this activity.

Phases of Matter Worksheet

Label which transition is most likely occurring during the following actions. Write your answers in the blanks provided.

Choose your answers from the words below:

melting point	sublimation	deposition	precipitation
condensation	freezing point	vaporization	evaporation

1. A burning candle: _____

2. A dripping ice cream cone: _____

3. A blizzard: _____

4. A frosty windshield: _____

5. A rainstorm: _____

6. Black storm clouds: _____

7. A dry ice machine: _____

8. Concentrated orange juice: _____

9. Evaporated milk: _____

How to Adapt This Lesson for the Inclusive Classroom

For Learning Disabled Students

Brainstorm very simple definitions of the terms listed below and make a word bank. The words can also be illustrated and labeled with assorted markers on note cards for a quick reference tool. Include the following terms:

condensation	melting point	transition
evaporation	solid	amorphous solid
sublimation	liquid	crystalline solid
freezing point	gas	precipitation

Students with learning disabilities may also benefit from playing What's the Matter? Use this game, designed for two to four players, to reinforce and review concepts presented in class.

What's the Matter?

1. Write the words Solid, Liquid, and Gas on note cards.

2. Place these cards on the table.

3. With a deck of blank note cards, colored pencils, and markers, assist the students in illustrating three pictures each of solids, liquids, and gases.

4. Place the illustrated cards in a deck and shuffle.

5. With the deck face down, begin by having each student pick a card and decide the category in which the illustration belongs. Students will then put the card next to the Solid, Liquid, or Gas card. If correct, the student receives one point.

6. Continue with players taking turns until all the cards are correctly placed. The student with the most points wins the game.

For Delayed Readers

Sometimes scientific terms can be difficult for students who struggle with reading skills. Aid students in decoding terms with multiple syllables in this activity by dividing the words into syllables and writing the phonetic as well as correct spellings on note cards. Place the definition of the word on the back of each card. Review pronunciation and definitions with the students orally. If students continue to struggle with words, rap the syllables on the desk with a pencil and have them model. This will aid in remembering the proper inflections in each word.

For Gifted Learners

Expand on this lesson by having students write and illustrate a young children's book explaining one or more of the phase transitions of matter. Students can place their books on display in the library; or, if possible, arrange a time during which students can read the books to a younger audience.

Whole Class Lab: Making Chocolate Candy

Purpose: This lab provides a practical example of a phase transition of matter. This lab works best with groups of two to four students.

Supplies (per group)
10-ounce bag of chocolate chips

candy mold

4-quart double boiler

wooden spoon

Pyrex measuring cup with a spout

oven mitts

plate

1. Have each group of students place chocolate chips in the top pot of the double boiler and fill the bottom with 1 cup of water. They then heat the water over a low flame until the chocolate is melted, turn off the stove, and stir with a wooden spoon.

2. With oven mitts, each group then takes the top pot off of their double boiler and carefully pours the melted chocolate into the measuring cup. Then have students pour liquid chocolate into the candy mold, which they then place in the freezer for twenty minutes.

3. After twenty minutes have elapsed, have students take the mold out of freezer and turn it over on a plate to release chocolate from the mold.

4. Ask students to write one-page essays with their respective groups explaining the various matter changes that occurred during this lab.

How to Adapt This Lab for the Inclusive Classroom

For Students with Fine Motor or Perceptual Difficulties

Assist students when pouring hot melted chocolate into the molds to minimize mess and prevent accidents.

For Learning Disabled Students or Students with Memory Weaknesses

Allow students to use notes from class to review phase transitions while writing their lab essays.

For Students with Physical Disabilities

The wheelchair-bound student can pour chocolate into the candy mold easily if a cutting board is placed across the wheelchair to create a flat work surface.

Home/School Connection

Give students the following assignment to complete at home:

Have your family help you design a three-dimensional collage of places in nature that showcase various states and phases of matter. Use photos from magazines, newspapers, or the Internet, and from such items as a shoe box, a coffee can, and so on. Bring the finished collage to class to display.

How to Evaluate This Lesson

We recommend a traditional assessment for this lesson. The teacher can type the following quiz and hand it out to the students to complete:

Phases of Matter Quiz

1. The process in which gas turns into a solid is called: _____.

2. Another word for rain is: _____.

3. An example of a liquid is: _____.

4. Condensation occurs when: _____.

5. Dry ice is an example of a: _____.

6. An example of a solid is: _____.

7. Vaporization occurs when: _____.

Activity 5: Acids and Bases

Purpose: Students will learn to determine whether a solution is acidic, basic, or neutral, and will become familiar with the pH scale.

Read through the lesson and the adaptations and make sure you have the supplies you will need.

Supplies for the main lesson

chalkboard, overhead projector, computer with presentation software, or interactive whiteboard

science notebooks

Supplies for the adaptations

highlighters

copies of notes

Lesson

1. Begin by saying something like, "Today we will discuss buffer solutions and how to determine whether they are acidic or basic. Who has heard those words before and wants to share what they know?"

2. Following a class discussion on the meaning of the words, write the following notes on the board and have students copy the definitions into their notebooks:

   a. **Solution:** A solution is a homogeneous mixture composed of two substances, one dissolved in the other. *Homogeneous* means the substance contains only one compound or element.

   b. **pH:** pH stands for power of hydrogen. The pH scale is a unit for measuring the hydrogen activity in solutions, determining how acidic or basic a solution is.

   c. **Acid:** An acid is any chemical compound that, when dissolved in water, yields a solution with a hydrogen activity greater than in pure water (pH less than 7.0). Acids have the following characteristics:

      - taste sour (but don't taste them!)

      - change litmus paper from blue to red

      Note that common acids include ascorbic acid (which can be found in fruits and vegetables), citric acid (which contains vitamin C), carbonic acid (which is used along with CO_2 in carbonation), and vinegar.

   c. **Base:** Any chemical compound that, when dissolved in water, gives a solution with a pH higher than 7.0 is a base. Bases have the following characteristics:

      - taste bitter (but don't taste them!)

      - feel slippery or soapy (but don't touch them!)

      - change litmus paper from red to blue

      Note that common bases include detergents, soap, lye, and ammonia.

d. **Neutral:** A substance that is neither an acid nor a base is considered neutral, having a balance between protons and hydroxide (OH–). An example of a neutral solution is water. A reaction between an acid and base is called neutralization.

Hand out the Acids and Bases Worksheet and proceed to work with small groups of students on some of the adaptations. Also, if time permits, have the students participate in the Whole Class Lab at the end of this activity.

Acids and Bases Worksheet

Choose the correct answer.

1. Tastes sour:
         a. Acid   b. Base   c. Neutral

2. Turns litmus paper blue:
         a. Acid   b. Base   c. Neutral

3. Feels slippery:
         a. Acid   b. Base   c. Neutral

4. Has a pH level less than 7.0:
         a. Acid   b. Base   c. Neutral

5. Has a balance between protons and hydroxide:
         a. Acid   b. Base   c. Neutral

6. Water is an example of a(n):
         a. Acid   b. Base   c. Neutral

7. List a few common examples of acids.

   _____

   _____

   _____

   _____

8. List a few common examples of bases.

   _____

   _____

   _____

   _____

How to Adapt This Lesson for the Inclusive Classroom

For Learning Disabled Students

Have these students review acids and bases using their notes. Students may also color code their own pH scales for future reference. Encourage students to refer to their scales to help them complete their worksheets.

For Students with Visual or Perceptual Difficulties

Use a graphic organizer to help them visually organize the information by comparing and contrasting the different characteristics of acids and bases.

Comparison of Acids and Bases

	Acids	Bases
Characteristic I	pH less than 7.0	pH more than 7.0
Characteristic II	Tastes sour (Do not taste!)	Tastes bitter (Do not taste!)
Characteristic III	Changes blue litmus paper to red	Changes red litmus paper to blue
Examples	Vitamin C Carbonic Acid Vinegar	Detergents Soaps Lye Ammonia

For Students with Memory Weaknesses

Students may visit the "GEMS Alien Juice Bar" at http://scienceview.berkeley.edu/show case/flash/juicebar.html for practice with identifying acids, bases, and neutral substances. They can also use mnemonic devices to help them remember these concepts, such as the one below:

BASE	ACID
B = Bitter.	**A** = A pH less than 7.0
A = Ammonia.	**C** = Changes litmus paper from red to blue
S = Slippery.	**I** = is part of vitamin C and vinegar
E = Every one has a pH over 7.0.	**D** = Do not taste—Sour!

For Students with Fine Motor Difficulties

Pass out copies of the notes that they can highlight as you go through the lesson.

For Gifted Learners

Expand on this lesson by having gifted learners create a pH scale for the classroom that the whole class can use for reference and on which the gifted learners can place common examples of acids and bases. Magazines or drawings may be used.

Whole Class Lab: Cabbage Juice Indicator

Purpose: In this lab, students will test household solutions with litmus paper, using red cabbage juice indicator; they will classify household substances as acids or bases.

This lab works best if students are in groups of four to six.

Supplies (per group)

container of red cabbage juice (make this in advance)

- Chop one large red cabbage into small pieces. (Blackberries, red onions, or hibiscus flowers can be used as substitutes.)
- Simmer the cabbage pieces until the water turns a deep shade of purple.
- Allow the water to cool and refrigerate when not in use.

red and blue litmus paper

seven plastic cups

beakers of the following solutions that you have made ahead of time: water, baking soda and water, vinegar, salt water, sugar water, lemon juice

black marker

1. Explain to students that red cabbage water is an indicator of pH. Although it can't be used to determine exact pH, it can distinguish between an acid (pH of 0 to 6), a neutral (pH near 7), and a base (pH of 8 to 14).

   Write the following on the board and explain it to students ahead of time:

   If the indicator turns the solution red or pink, the solution is an acid; a purple solution indicates that it is neutral, neither an acid nor a base; and if the indicator turns the solution blue or green, the solution is a base.

How to Read pH Paper

Red litmus paper:

    Stays red = acid or neutral

    Turns blue = base

Blue litmus paper:

    Stays blue = base or neutral

    Turns red = acid

2. Have students label their plastic cups as follows: water, baking soda, vinegar, salt water, sugar water, and lemon juice.

3. Students then pour a small amount of each solution into the labeled plastic cups.

4. Have each group of students place a drop of each solution onto a separate piece of red and then blue litmus paper and record the results in their data table (included below).

5. Each group then adds 1 to 2 tablespoons of red cabbage juice to the solution cup labeled "water," and records the color change in the data table.

6. Students are to determine whether the solution is acidic, basic, or neutral and to write the answers in the data table. Reproduce the data table below for the students.

7. Students then repeat steps 5 and 6 using the other solutions.

Data Table

Solution	Red Litmus	Blue Litmus	Red Cabbage Juice	Acid, Base, or Neutral
Water				
Baking Soda and Water				
Vinegar				
Salt Water				
Sugar Water				
Lemon Juice				

8. Ask students to write two to three sentences about what they learned, including why it is important to use both blue and red litmus paper to determine pH.

How to Adapt This Lab for the Inclusive Classroom

For Students with Physical Disabilities or Fine Motor Difficulties

For the wheelchair-bound student, place a cutting board across the wheelchair to give an ample work surface for the student. Also, students may require assistance from paraprofessionals while wetting litmus paper or pouring the cabbage juice.

For Learning Disabled Students

Make sure these students have a pH scale for reference. A pH scale places common items along a pH continuum. A variety of these are available in textbooks, pet stores, or via the Internet. They may also summarize their findings orally or using diagrams.

For Students with Behavioral Difficulties or ADD/ADHD

Place their groups near your desk so you can help keep them on track. Make sure to balance these groups with students possessing strong collaborative group skills.

Home/School Connection

Give students the following assignment to complete at home:

> Work with a parent and compile a list of many common acids, bases, and neutral substances found in your home. Bring this list to school to share.

How to Evaluate This Lesson

Use students' work—including a combination of the worksheet, lab findings, and Home/School Connection—to assess their understanding.

Activity 6: Using the Periodic Table

Purpose: Students will use the periodic table to identify elements in simple compounds. They should learn to use the periodic table as a quick reference for associating the name and symbol of an element in compounds and ions. They should also be able to find the atomic number and atomic weight of a given element listed on the table.

Read through the lesson and the adaptations and make sure you have the supplies you will need.

Supplies for the main lesson

large, class-size periodic table

chalkboard, overhead projector, computer with presentation software, or interactive whiteboard

science notebooks

Supplies for the adaptations

highlighters

student-created elements card decks

individual periodic tables

copies of notes

Lesson

1. Hang a large, class-size periodic table where everyone can see it.

2. Start by saying something like, "Today we will begin a discussion about the periodic table. Who can share what they know about it?"

3. Following a class discussion, say, "Now I'm going to tell you the story of how the periodic table came to be. Dmitri Mendeleev, a Russian scientist who was born in 1834, is known as the creator of the periodic table of the elements. Mendeleev noticed that patterns appeared when the known elements were arranged in order of increasing atomic mass, which is the mass of a single atom. Arranging the elements by increasing atomic mass left three blank spaces in the table. Mendeleev suggested that elements that had yet to be discovered would fill these blank spots. This first periodic table was published in 1869. The word 'periodic' refers to a repeating pattern: in this case, the properties of the elements repeat with each row—or period—of the table."

   "Only sixteen years later, chemists discovered the three missing elements (scandium, gallium, and germanium) and found that their properties were very close to what Mendeleev had predicted."

4. Explain that the periodic table is both a tool and an organized arrangement of the elements that reveals the underlying atomic structure of the atoms. Each box represents a different element, and contains important information about that element: name, symbol, atomic number, and atomic mass.

5. Explain the following features of the periodic table and write them on the board, having students copy them down in their notebooks:

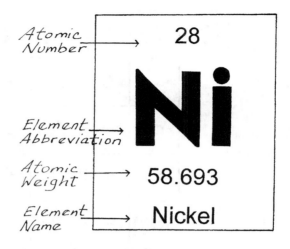

a. **Groups or Families:** The eighteen vertical columns in the periodic table show the groups or families of elements. Elements in the same family or group have similar characteristics. All of the elements in a family have the same number of electrons (which carry a negative electric charge) in their outer shells. You can predict the properties of a certain element by knowing the group to which it belongs.

b. **Periods:** The horizontal rows in the periodic table show the periods. Elements in a period are not alike in their properties. Atomic size decreases from left to right across a period, but atomic mass increases from left to right across a period. Atoms on the left of the period are usually larger and more lightweight than the smaller, heavier atoms on the right.

c. **Atomic Number:** The number at the top of each element's box is its atomic number. The atomic number is the number of protons (which carry a positive electric charge) in the nucleus of an atom of that element.

d. **Atomic Mass:** The number at the bottom of each element's box is its atomic mass. Atomic mass is the average mass of atoms of that element.

Hand out the Periodic Table Worksheet and proceed to work with small groups of students on some of the adaptations. Also, if time permits, have the students participate in the Whole Class Lab at the end of this activity.

Periodic Table

Z	Symbol	Atomic Mass	Name
1	H	1.007	Hydrogen
2	He	4.002	Helium
3	Li	6.941	Lithium
4	Be	9.012	Beryllium
5	B	10.811	Boron
6	C	12.011	Carbon
7	N	14.001	Nitrogen
8	O	15.999	Oxygen
9	F	18.998	Fluorine
10	Ne	20.180	Neon
11	Na	22.990	Sodium
12	Mg	24.305	Magnesium
13	Al	26.982	Aluminium
14	Si	28.085	Silicon
15	P	30.974	Phosphorus
16	S	32.065	Sulfur
17	Cl	35.453	Chlorine
18	Ar	39.948	Argon
19	K	39.098	Potassium
20	Ca	40.078	Calcium
21	Sc	44.945	Scandium
22	Ti	47.867	Titanium
23	V	50.941	Vanadium
24	Cr	51.996	Chromium
25	Mn	54.938	Manganese
26	Fe	55.845	Iron
27	Co	58.933	Cobalt
28	Ni	58.693	Nickel
29	Cu	63.546	Copper
30	Zn	65.409	Zinc
31	Ga	69.723	Gallium
32	Ge	72.64	Germanium
33	As	74.922	Arsenic
34	Se	78.96	Selenium
35	Br	79.904	Bromine
36	Kr	83.798	Krypton
37	Rb	85.468	Rubidium
38	Sr	87.62	Strontium
39	Y	88.906	Yttrium
40	Zr	91.224	Zirconium
41	Nb	92.906	Niobium
42	Mo	95.94	Molybdenum
43	Tc	98	Technetium
44	Ru	101.07	Ruthenium
45	Rh	102.906	Rhodium
46	Pd	106.42	Palladium
47	Ag	107.868	Silver
48	Cd	112.411	Cadmium
49	In	114.818	Indium
50	Sn	118.710	Tin
51	Sb	121.760	Antimony
52	Te	127.60	Tellurium
53	I	126.904	Iodine
54	Xe	131.294	Xenon
55	Cs	132.905	Caesium
56	Ba	137.327	Barium
57–71			Lanthanoids
72	Hf	178.49	Hafnium
73	Ta	180.948	Tantalum
74	W	183.84	Tungsten
75	Re	186.207	Rhenium
76	Os	190.23	Osmium
77	Ir	192.217	Iridium
78	Pt	195.084	Platinum
79	Au	196.967	Gold
80	Hg	200.59	Mercury
81	Tl	204.383	Thallium
82	Pb	207.2	Lead
83	Bi	208.980	Bismuth
84	Po	209	Polonium
85	At	210	Astatine
86	Rn	222	Radon
87	Fr	223	Francium
88	Ra	226	Radium
89–103			Actinoids
104	Rf	261	Rutherfordium
105	Db	262	Dubnium
106	Sg	266	Seaborgium
107	Bh	264	Bohrium
108	Hs	277	Hassium
109	Mt	268	Meitnerium
110	Ds	271	Darmstadtium
111	Rg	272	Roentgenium
112	Uub		Ununbium
113	Uut		Ununtrium
114	Uuq		Ununquadium
115	Uup		Ununpentium
116	Uuh		Ununhexium
117	Uus		Ununseptium
118	Uuo		Ununoctium

Lanthanoids

Z	Symbol	Atomic Mass	Name
57	La	138.905	Lanthanum
58	Ce	140.116	Cerium
59	Pr	140.908	Praseodymium
60	Nd	144.242	Neodymium
61	Pm	145	Promethium
62	Sm	150.36	Samarium
63	Eu	151.964	Europium
64	Gd	157.25	Gadolinium
65	Tb	158.925	Terbium
66	Dy	162.500	Dysprosium
67	Ho	164.930	Holmium
68	Er	167.259	Erbium
69	Tm	168.934	Thulium
70	Yb	173.04	Ytterbium
71	Lu	174.967	Lutetium

Actinoids

Z	Symbol	Atomic Mass	Name
89	Ac	227	Actinium
90	Th	232.038	Thulium
91	Pa	231.036	Protactinium
92	U	238.029	Uranium
93	Np	237	Neptunium
94	Pu	244	Plutonium
95	Am	243	Americium
96	Cm	247	Curium
97	Bk	247	Berkelium
98	Cf	251	Californium
99	Es	252	Einsteinium
100	Fm	257	Fermium
101	Md	258	Mendelevium
102	No	259	Nobelium
103	Lr	262	Lawrencium

Name: _____   Date: _____

Periodic Table Worksheet

Answer the following questions.

1. The horizontal rows of the periodic table are called:

   a. rows

   b. lines

   c. periods

2. The columns of the periodic table are called:

   a. groups or families

   b. periodicals

   c. elements

3. All of the elements in a period have the same:

   a. atomic weight

   b. number of atomic shells

   c. color

4. All of the elements in a family or group have the same number of:

   a. neutrons

   b. molecules

   c. electrons in their outer shells

5. The atomic number of a given element represents:

   a. the number of electrons in an atom of that element

   b. the number of protons in the nucleus of an atom

   c. the number of shells belonging to an atom

6. The atomic mass of a given element represents:

   a. the number of electrons in an atom of that element

   b. the mass of one atom

   c. the mass of one of the protons

7. Fill in the element name on the blank line and label the atomic mass and atomic number.

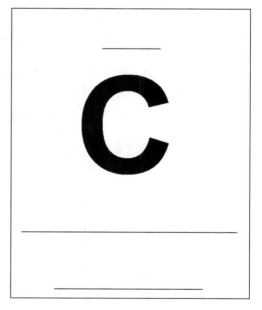

79

How to Adapt This Lesson for the Inclusive Classroom

For Learning Disabled Students

Review and reteach concepts relating to the periodic table. Students may also color code their own periodic tables for future reference. Each student can color each vertical column a different color to illustrate that these are the families or groups that share characteristics. Encourage students to refer to the periodic table to help them complete the worksheet.

For Students with Memory Weaknesses

Students can play a memory games or quiz each other using the element cards as flashcards. They can also create songs or mnemonics to help with remembering the concepts pertaining to the periodic table.

For Students with Fine Motor or Perceptual Difficulties

Pass out copies of your notes for them to highlight as you give the lesson. Also, be sure to have a large, easy-to-see periodic table posted in the classroom.

For Gifted Learners

Expand on this lesson by having students do a research project on how the periodic table is used by scientists in different fields. For example, astrophysicists use a table that includes elemental abundances in the solar system, physicists and engineers use tables that include boiling and melting points or thermal and electrical conductivity of the elements, and chemists use tables that show the electron structures of the elements.

Whole Class Lab: Marshmallow Molecules!

Purpose: This lab will help students understand the structures of molecules.

Students work in groups of 4.

Supplies

box of toothpicks

colored mini-marshmallows

1. Explain that molecular shapes give scientists information on how compounds might react and why. Without this information, chemists would not be able to make the amazing advances that are accomplished each day.

2. Have marshmallows represent the following atoms:
   - Pink marshmallows represent hydrogen.
   - Orange marshmallows represent oxygen.
   - Yellow marshmallows represent carbon.
   - Green marshmallows represent chlorine.

3. Toothpicks should represent the bonds between the atoms.

4. Have the students make the following molecules using the marshmallows and toothpicks and draw a picture of each.

$$H_2O \qquad HCl \qquad C_6H_{12}O_6 \qquad CO_2 \qquad CH_4$$

5. Challenge students to match the molecules with their names: hydrochloric acid, water, carbon dioxide, glucose, and methane. Have them hand in pictures and models at the end of the lab.

How to Adapt This Lab for the Inclusive Classroom

For Students with Physical Disabilities or Fine Motor Difficulties

For the wheelchair-bound student, place a cutting board across the wheelchair to give the student an ample work surface. Also, these students may use larger marshmallows. Have them show you their three-dimensional representations and skip the drawing component, if that is too great a challenge.

For Learning Disabled Students

Make sure they have a periodic table for reference in order to associate the symbol and name of each element.

For Students with Behavioral Difficulties or ADD/ADHD

Place these students in groups near your desk so you can help keep them on track. Make sure to balance their groups with students possessing strong collaborative skills.

Home/School Connection

Give students the following assignment to complete at home:

Choose an element and create an 8½- by 11-inch element poster that shows the basic information about the element, including its common uses. Ask family members to help research the common uses for your element.

How to Evaluate This Lesson

Use students' work—including the worksheet, marshmallow molecules (three-dimensional figures and drawings), and Home/School Connection—to assess their understanding.

Activity 7: Alternative Energy Sources

Purpose: This activity will teach students about different types of natural energy, such as wind power, fossil fuels, hydropower, and solar power. Students will learn to classify these energy sources as renewable or nonrenewable.

Read through the lesson and the adaptations and make sure you have the supplies you will need.

Supplies for the main lesson

chalkboard, overhead projector, computer with presentation software, or interactive whiteboard

science notebooks

pinwheel

glass of water

picture of the sun

Supplies for the adaptations

highlighters

copies of notes

index cards

Lesson

1. Before discussing the specifics of renewable sources of energy, grab the students' attention by holding up a pinwheel, a glass of water, and a picture of the sun. Ask the students, "What do these have in common?" Explain that they all represent alternative energy sources: wind power, hydropower, and solar power.

2. Then say, "Now let's talk about alternative energy sources. Let's see what we already know."

3. Following a class discussion, write the following notes on the board and have students copy them down in their notebooks:

   a. **Renewable Resource:** A natural resource that is depleted at a rate slower than the rate at which it regenerates, such as solar energy, is a renewable resource.

   b. **Nonrenewable Resource:** Resources for which there are no ways to replenish the supply, such as fossil fuels, are nonrenewable.

   c. **Fossil Fuels:** Also known as mineral fuels, fossil fuels are natural resources containing hydrocarbons, such as coal, petroleum, and natural gas.

   d. **Solar Energy:** Harnessing the energy produced by sunlight produces solar energy.

   e. **Wind Power:** Motion energy, or kinetic energy, of the wind or wind turbines is used to extract the wind's energy, making use of wind power.

   f. **Hydropower:** Hydropower is energy obtained from flowing water.

g. **Geothermal Energy:** Electricity generated by utilizing naturally occurring geological heat sources is a form of geothermal energy.

h. **Hydrogen Fuel Cells:** Hydrogen fuel cells are electrochemical cells in which the energy of a reaction between fuels—for example, between liquid hydrogen and an oxidant, such as liquid oxygen—is converted into electrical energy.

i. **Nuclear Energy:** Energy released from the nucleus of an atom that creates a nuclear reaction is called nuclear energy.

4. Then say, "There are two types of nonrenewable energy in the list we just went over. Can anyone share what those are?" Explain that these are fossil fuels and nuclear energy.

Hand out the Alternative Energy Sources Worksheet and proceed to work with small groups of students on some of the adaptations. Also, if time permits, have the students participate in the Whole Class Lab at the end of this activity.

Alternative Energy Sources Worksheet

Answer the following questions.

1. What does it mean when an energy resource is said to be "renewable"?

   _____

   _____

   _____

2. What does it mean when an energy resource is said to be "nonrenewable"?

   _____

   _____

   _____

3. Give three or more examples of renewable energy resources.

   _____

   _____

   _____

4. Give three or more examples of nonrenewable energy resources.

   _____

   _____

   _____

5. What are "fossil fuels"?

   _____

   _____

   _____

How to Adapt This Lesson for the Inclusive Classroom

For Learning Disabled Students

Review the lesson notes. Students may use a graphic organizer to help them visually organize the information, separating renewable and nonrenewable energy sources. They can use this organizer to complete the worksheet.

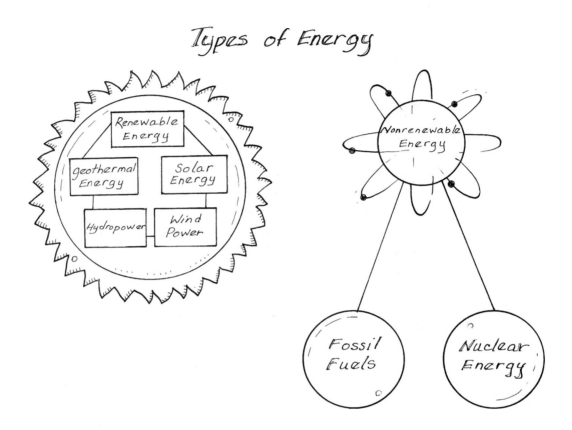

For Students with Memory Weaknesses

Students may make flashcards to help them remember the different types of energy. These flashcards will each include the definition of the type of energy on one side, and a picture or a memory clue on the other. Students can quiz each other for mastery.

For Students with Fine Motor or Perceptual Difficulties

Pass out copies of the notes that they can highlight as you give the lesson. Students can also use a computer to type out and print the answers to their worksheets, and staple these to their worksheets.

For Gifted Learners

Expand on this lesson by having students first research the pros and cons of hybrid cars, and then ask their parents if they would purchase one for the family and why or why not. Have these students write persuasive speeches for or against hybrid cars and present them to the class. They should think about, for example, such issues as whether hybrid cars demonstrate a good use of science or are simply a short-term solution to delay the inevitable depletion of fossil fuel resources, or the extent to which hybrid vehicles improve the environment.

Whole Class Lab: Message in a Bottle

Purpose: This lab demonstrates one of the reasons to pursue alternative sources of energy by allowing students to create smog in a bottle.

Have students work in pairs.

Supplies (per pair)

2-liter bottle with its top cut off

warm water

matches (not for student use)

small plastic bag filled with ice

1. Start by saying to the class, "One problem with such traditional energy sources as coal, oil, and gas is that they produce gases and small particles that can foul the air and produce smog when tiny droplets of water condense around them."
2. Have each pair put some ice cubes in a small plastic bag.
3. Students then pour an inch or two of warm water into their bottles.
4. Light a match and hold it inside each pair's bottle for a second, and then drop the match into the water.
5. Have each pair close the top of their bottle with the small plastic bag. Students then watch the smog form inside as the warm, wet, smoky air rises up to touch the cold plastic bag.
6. Students should count to thirty seconds before taking the plastic bag off the top and watching the smog rise into the air. If it's a sunny day, have students work near a window where the sun can shine in and light up the smog.
7. Ask students to write two to three sentences on their findings and to comment on why they think scientists should pursue alternative energy sources.

How to Adapt This Lab for the Inclusive Classroom

For Students with Physical Disabilities or Fine Motor Difficulties

For the wheelchair-bound student, place a cutting board across the wheelchair to create an ample work surface.

For Learning Disabled Students

Before starting the lab, provide them with a model of the finished product to look at as well as printed directions that they may reference. These students may also summarize their findings orally or with diagrams.

For Students with Behavioral Difficulties or ADD/ADHD

Place their pairs near your desk so you can help keep them on track. Make sure to balance their pairs with students possessing strong collaborative group skills.

Home/School Connection

Have students complete the following assignment at home:

Discuss solar panels for heating your home with your parents. Together, determine whether it is something you would be interested in or not. If solar panels are not a good option for your home, discuss what might be a possible alternative. Bring in your finding to share with the class. This data could be distributed on a bar graph.

How to Evaluate This Lesson

Use students' work—including the worksheet, lab findings, and Home/School Connection—to assess their understanding.

Chapter 6

Earth and Space Science

Activity 1: Types of Rocks

Purpose: Students will understand and learn to identify the three basic rock types.

Read through the lesson and the adaptations and make sure you have the supplies you will need.

Supplies for the main lesson

chalkboard, overhead projector, computer with presentation software, or interactive whiteboard

science notebooks

Internet access

Supplies for the adaptations

index cards

three different colored markers

examples of types of rocks

plain white paper

Lesson

1. Begin by saying something like, "Today we are going to learn about three basic types of rocks. They are igneous, sedimentary, and metamorphic rocks."

2. Write the following definitions on the board and have students copy them down in their notebooks:

   a. **Igneous Rocks:** Igneous rocks come from the cooled magma from volcanic eruptions. There are two types:

      Intrusive Igneous Rocks: These are rocks that form when the magma or molten rock goes through the volcanoes. It later becomes lava when it cools beneath the earth's surface. These rocks intrude into the existing rocks and are visible because of erosion. Granite is an example of an intrusive igneous rock. Other examples include diorite and pumice.

      Extrusive Igneous Rocks: When magma reaches the earth's surface, it is called lava. An extrusive igneous rock is formed when the lava cools and hardens. Examples of extrusive igneous rocks are rhyolite, andesite, and basalt.

   b. **Sedimentary Rocks:** Sedimentary rocks are formed when solids settle out of either a fluid, such as the water in oceans or rivers, or air. These solids or sediments combine to form sedimentary rocks. There are two types:

      Clastic Sedimentary Rocks: Clastic sedimentary rocks are made from bits of rocks and minerals that are compacted together. An example of a clastic sedimentary rock is quartz. Other examples are siltstone, sandstone, and shale.

Chemical Sedimentary Rocks: Chemical sedimentary rocks are formed when the solids separate from evaporated water. An example of a chemical sedimentary rock is limestone. Other examples are flint and gypsum.

c. **Metamorphic Rocks:** Metamorphic rocks are igneous or sedimentary rocks that have been changed by heat, water, and pressure. Usually these three change agents are present at the same time, causing the rock's substance to change form. There are two types of metamorphic rocks:

Foliated Metamorphic Rocks: These rocks have been under such extreme conditions that the change in structure results in a rock with a layered appearance. An example of a foliated metamorphic rock is gneiss, which comes from shale.

Nonfoliated Metamorphic Rocks: A nonfoliated metamorphic rock is smooth. It does not develop layers or bands after exposure to heat and pressure. An example of a nonfoliated metamorphic rock is marble, which comes from limestone.

Hand out the Types of Rocks and Their Uses Worksheet and proceed to work with small groups of students on some of the adaptations. Also, if time permits, have the students participate in the Whole Class Lab at the end of this activity.

Types of Rocks and Their Uses Worksheet

In small groups, use your class notes to fill in the answers to the sentences below. Conduct research on the Web to find out various uses for different rocks.

1. Rocks that form when magma cools below the earth's surface are called: _____

   _____.

2. _____ is an example of an intrusive igneous rock.

3. A rock that changes as a result of heat, water, and pressure is called a: _____

   _____.

4. _____ are formed when solids separate from

   evaporated water.

5. The three main types of rocks are: _____,

   _____, and _____.

6. Name some uses for these rocks:

   a. quartz: _____   f. limestone: _____

   b. sandstone: _____   g. gneiss: _____

   c. shale: _____   h. basalt: _____

   d. marble: _____   i. pumice: _____

   e. granite: _____   j. rhyolite: _____

How to Adapt This Lesson for the Inclusive Classroom

For Learning Disabled Students

Model how to look up the uses of rocks on the Internet. Work with students in finding the answers.

Using notes from class, have students write definitions of the three types and sub-types of rocks on index cards in different colored markers. This would makes filling out the worksheet easier, because the notes would be condensed.

Have students make a display of different rocks and their uses in order to reinforce their understanding of rock uses and the related concepts. These students might also benefit from a graphic organizer illustrating the types of rocks and their uses, which would aid them when studying for tests.

For Students with Fine Motor or Perceptual Difficulties

Allow these students to copy notes from this lesson ahead of time, which they then can use as study guides for test-taking purposes.

For Gifted Learners

Expand on this lesson by having gifted learners work in a small group to develop a Jeopardy Rocks game, including all the information about rocks and their uses covered in class and on the worksheet. When finished, the group can present the game to the class as a review.

Whole Class Lab: Making Rock Candy

Purpose: This experiment is designed to show students a real-life example of how heat and water can change a substance, similar to the process by which a metamorphic rock is created.

Divide students into small groups of four or five, supervising each group yourself or with the help of a paraprofessional, classroom aide, or parent. This lab requires the use of a room with a stove or a burner, such as a cafeteria or life skills room.

Supplies (per group)

4 cups of sugar

2 cups of water

small saucepan

wooden spoon

small, clean glass jar

cotton string

weight to hang on the string (such as a washer)

waxed paper

1. Have students add sugar and water to their saucepans, and supervise them while they heat the pans at medium-high heat, stirring constantly until the sugar comes to a rolling boil. Students then turn off the heat and add a few drops of food coloring to the mixtures.

2. Carefully pour each group's solution into their glass jar. Students should cover the jar with waxed paper until they are ready to use the solution.

3. Have each group tie a weight, such as a washer, to one end of the cotton string, tying the other end to the middle of a pencil. The string should be long enough that the weight hangs a little above the bottom of the jar when the pencil is rested on the top of the jar. Students then put the string in the sugar solution until it is soaked, and lay it stretched out on a piece of waxed paper to dry for a few days.

4. After the necessary time has elapsed, have each group place the prepared string in the solution and watch their crystals grow before their eyes! This process usually takes about a week. Make sure that students do not eat the finished rock candy.

How to Adapt This Lab for the Inclusive Classroom

For Students with Physical Disabilities

Be sure to pay careful attention to these students when they are near the stove.

Home/School Connection

Give students the following assignment to complete at home:

Using pictures from the Internet, newspapers, and/or magazines, make a collage of different types of rocks and label them with their names and uses.

How to Evaluate This Lesson

Prepare a traditional quiz, similar in format to the worksheet that covers different types of rocks and their uses.

Activity 2: Volcanoes

Purpose: Students will be able to identify the types of volcanoes and understand the primary reasons why volcanoes erupt.

Read through the lesson and the adaptations and make sure you have the supplies you will need.

Supplies for the main lesson

chalkboard, overhead projector, computer with presentation software, or interactive whiteboard

picture examples of composite volcanoes, shield volcanoes, and cinder cone volcanoes

science notebooks

Supplies for the adaptations

colored construction paper

scissors

computer paper

overhead projector with presentation software

funnels

Lesson

1. Start by saying something like, "Today we are going to learn about three main types of volcanoes and why volcanoes erupt. The three main types of volcanoes are composite volcanoes, shield volcanoes, and cinder cone volcanoes."

2. Write the following notes on the board and display the pictures of the three main types of volcanoes, having students copy the definitions down in their notebooks:

   a. **Composite Volcanoes:** A composite volcano is a large, cone-like structure that is the product of gaseous magma and generates very viscous (thick) lava. Composite volcanoes are the most beautiful and the most dangerous volcanoes, because they have the most explosive eruptions. Found primarily in what is called the "Ring of Fire," which is located near the islands in the Northern and Western Pacific Ocean, some famous composite volcanoes include Mount Rainier and Mount St. Helens in Washington State and Mount Fuji in Japan.

   b. **Shield Volcanoes:** Shield volcanoes have been produced from volcanic rock that has hardened from lava. Many have grown from the ocean floor and formed islands. Examples of shield volcanoes include those on the big island of Hawaii.

   c. **Cinder Cone Volcanoes:** A cinder cone volcano usually forms a steep slope and is made from a single volcanic eruption. Ejected lava fragments, or "cinders," harden in the air and form the cone-shaped volcano. These volcanoes usually have a short life span and resemble craters. They also occur in groupings and can form the sides of larger volcanoes. Mount Etna is an example of a volcano with many cinder cones.

3. Next discuss the three main types of volcanic materials, saying, "Three main materials make up the substance that extrudes from volcanoes when they erupt. They are lava, gases, and pyroclastic materials." Write the following notes on the board and have students copy them down in their notebooks:

   a. **Lava:** Lava is molten rock. It erupts from a volcano and is extremely hot, with temperatures as high as 2,000 degrees Fahrenheit. Lava takes a long time to cool. When it does, it forms igneous rock.

   b. **Gases:** Common gases in a volcano mix with the lava. With pressure, these gases escape and aid in creating a volcanic explosion. Common gases in molten lava are carbon dioxide and sulfur dioxide.

   c. **Pyroclastic Materials:** Pyroclastic materials include rocks, glass fragments, and debris, which are blown out of the volcano in varying shapes and sizes.

4. Now talk about why volcanoes erupt, saying, "Volcanoes erupt when the pressure in the magma below the earth's surface becomes more intense than the structure of the volcano can contain. The pressure, gases, molten rock, and particles need to expand. If the pressure is released easily then the explosion will be a quiet one, such as in a shield volcano or on the main island of Hawaii. If the pressure is released violently, you will have a dangerous explosion, such as that from Mount St. Helens."

Hand out the Volcanoes Worksheet and proceed to work with small groups of students on some of the adaptations. Also, if time permits, have the students participate in the Whole Class Lab at the end of this activity.

Name: _____   Date: _____

Volcanoes Worksheet

Circle the best possible answer for each question.

1. The Ring of Fire is located in:
   a. the Northern and Western Pacific Ocean
   b. Mount Fuji, Japan
   c. Mount Etna
   d. Iceland

2. An example of a composite volcano is:
   a. Mount Rushmore
   b. Mount St. Helens
   c. molten rock
   d. lava

3. Shield volcanoes are often:
   a. explosive
   b. craters
   c. islands
   d. eruptions

4. A volcano made from a single volcanic eruption is called a:
   a. shield volcano
   b. composite volcano
   c. cinder cone volcano
   d. Ring of Fire

5. Another word for molten rock is:
   a. igneous rock
   b. sulfur dioxide
   c. carbon dioxide
   d. lava

Define the following terms

6. Lava:

   _____

   _____

7. Gases:

   _____

   _____

8. Pyroclastic Materials:

   _____

   _____

9. In your own words, explain how a volcano erupts.

   _____

   _____

   _____

   _____

How to Adapt This Lesson for the Inclusive Classroom

For Learning Disabled Students

Review the notes presented in class in a small group to reinforce the lesson. Provide students with partial notes (see illustration). Then model a self-talk strategy to aid in answering multiple choice questions (see example on page 99).

I. Volcanoes—Types

a) Composite Volcanoes—A large, cone-like structure that is the product of gaseous magma. This volcano generates lava. Example: ——————.

b) Shield Volcanoes — Shield volcanoes have been produced from volcanic rock that has hardened from ——————. Many have grown on the ocean floor and have formed ——————. Examples include ——————. and ——————.

c) Cinder Cone Volcano—

Example of a cinder cone volcano is ——————.

II. Volcanic Material

a) Lava

b) Gases

c) Pyroclastic Materials

Self-Talk Strategy for Multiple Choice Questions

First model this strategy for the students, and then have them repeat it themselves.

"Let's look at the first multiple choice question. I will read it aloud. The question is asking where the Ring of Fire is located. The answer I need to find is a place.

"Okay, now let's go through each of the answer choices. Answer 'a' says the Northern and Western Pacific Ocean. That answer is pretty broad. Broad answers may work here, because a Ring of Fire sounds like it may include more than one place. I think I'll check my notes. My notes say that the Ring of Fire is located near many islands, so I think my guess that more than one place is involved is correct. I need to check all the other answers first, because the directions say choose the best possible answer.

"Choice 'b' is a volcano. Mount Fuji is in Japan, but is only one site. I determined that the Ring of Fire is located near many islands, so Mount Fuji cannot be the best possible answer.

"Choices 'c' and 'd' are also single places. They are Mount Etna and Iceland. Both of these answers are also incorrect.

"Therefore, choice 'a,' which says the Ring of Fire is located in the Northern and Western Pacific Ocean, is correct."

Model the self-talk strategy with the remaining items on the worksheet.

For Students with Visual Difficulties

A colored bookmark, made from construction paper, may be used to cover other answer choices when answering the multiple choice questions. Also, explaining how a volcano erupts with a diagram will minimize the amount of text that students must read and study.

For Resistant Learners or Students with ADD/ADHD

If a student with behavioral difficulties is particularly distracted, pair him or her with another student to complete the worksheet. If the multiple choice questions seem difficult, the pair can utilize the self-talk strategy and take turns answering the questions.

For Gifted Learners

Expand on this lesson by having gifted learners research famous volcanoes, such as Mount St. Helens, Mount Vesuvius, Mona Loa, and Mount Fuji, and develop a PowerPoint presentation to give to the class.

Whole Class Lab: Classic Baking Soda Volcano

Purpose: This lab shows how a volcano erupts.

This experiment will work best if the class divides up into groups of three or four students.

Supplies (per group)

piece of cardboard, approximately 12 inches long

aluminum foil

plastic water bottle with cap

package of gray or brown modeling clay

warm water

5 drops of liquid dish detergent

3 drops each of red and yellow food coloring

3 tablespoons of baking soda

white vinegar

1-cup liquid measuring cup

lined paper

pencils

1. Have each group cover their cardboard with aluminum foil.
2. Students then fill their water bottles ¾ of the way with warm water. Next, they add 5 drops of dish detergent and 3 drops of food coloring, putting the cap on the water bottle and lightly shaking it.
3. Each group places their bottle on the cardboard, having one person hold the bottle while others shape a volcano base with modeling clay. Students should ensure that the bottle is secured in the clay.
4. Students then uncap their bottles. (It might be best, at this time, to move the experiment outside!) Have them add the two tablespoons of baking soda to the bottles. Students first pour approximately half a cup of vinegar into their measuring cups, before pouring the vinegar into their bottles and watching what happens!
5. Have each group jointly write a paragraph describing what happened and why they think it occurred.

How to Adapt This Lab for the Inclusive Classroom
For Students with Fine Motor or Perceptual Difficulties
These students can use funnels to help pour the liquids into the bottle.

Home/School Connection
Give students the following assignment to complete at home:

> Make a three-dimensional model of a famous volcano using modeling clay, papier mâché, or other materials. Fill out an index card with your volcano's name and five facts about it, including what type of volcano it is. Bring your model into class to display.

How to Evaluate This Lesson
Evaluate this lesson based on students' volcano models, worksheets, and class participation. If possible, meet individually with each student to discuss the pertinent facts about his or her volcano model.

Activity 3: Minerals

Purpose: This activity will help students understand and identify the properties of minerals and how they form.

Read through the lesson and the adaptations and make sure you have the supplies you will need.

Supplies for the main lesson

chalkboard, overhead projector, computer with presentation software, or interactive whiteboard

science notebooks

Supplies for the adaptations

unlined paper

colored markers

index cards

copies of notes

Lesson

1. Start by saying something like, "Today we are going to talk about various minerals and how they form. Minerals are naturally occurring, inorganic solids that are found in nature. An inorganic substance is a substance of mineral origin instead of plant origin.

   "Salt, nickel, copper, talc, limestone, calcium, feldspar, gold, iron, diamonds, and rubies are common examples of minerals that we see and use every day. Minerals have specific characteristics."

2. Write the following characteristics of minerals on the board and have students copy them down in their notebooks:

   a. They are naturally occurring.

   b. They have a defined chemical composition. Many minerals are made up of two or more elements.

   c. They have an orderly crystalline structure. Crystals must be arranged in a pattern that repeats itself. A diamond, for example, displays a repeated, crystalline structure.

   d. Minerals are usually inorganic. With the exception of salt, these are not the same minerals that are found in food.

   e. Minerals are solids.

3. Explain that minerals are formed in the earth, and that there are four major ways that minerals form: from magma, from changes in temperature and pressure, from precipitation, and from hydrothermal solutions. Write these ways on the board and have students copy them down in their notebooks:

a. **Magma:** Magma is molten rock formed below the earth's surface. As magma cools, elements in it combine to form minerals. Common minerals formed from magma are iron, magnesium, and calcium.

b. **Changes in Temperature and Pressure:** When existing minerals undergo changes in temperature and pressure, minerals recrystallize and form other minerals. Examples of minerals that develop in this way include amethyst, topaz, and calcite.

c. **Precipitation:** When water from lakes, rivers, and oceans evaporates, the dissolved substances in the water recrystallize to form minerals. Limestone, for example, is a mineral formed through precipitation.

d. **Hydrothermal Solutions:** Hydrothermal solutions are very hot mixtures of water and dissolved substances that come into contact with existing minerals and change their composition through a chemical reaction. An example of a mineral that experiences this type of reaction is quartz.

4. Explain that minerals have certain properties, and that these can be used to identify them. Write the following properties on the board and have students copy them down in their notebooks:

a. **Color:** You can see many different colors within a mineral.

b. **Streak:** This is the constant color that the mineral shows when rubbed against an abrasive surface.

c. **Luster:** Minerals shine like metal. An example of this is the shine on the facets or part of the surface of diamonds or quartz. All minerals have luster.

d. **Crystal Form:** Inside a mineral, a crystal form is visible. It will form into well-defined faces.

e. **Hardness:** Hardness can be determined by rubbing a mineral against another mineral. The standard used to determine hardness of minerals is called the Mohs' scale. This scale consists of ten minerals, arranged from softest to hardest. Any mineral of unknown hardness can be rubbed against another mineral to determine how hard it is, based on the order of the scale.

f. **Fracture:** Minerals break in specific ways. When the breakage is uneven, a fracture results. These breaks, however irregular, are still specific to the mineral. For example, a piece of quartz is very strong and will fracture evenly in all directions. This helps to identify the mineral as quartz.

g. **Cleavage:** Cleavage refers to the mineral's ability to break along even, flat surfaces.

h. **Density:** Minerals have a specific density. Density refers to how much mass is in a specific volume of that mineral, and explains how much matter is packed into one given space. For example, gold has a density of 19.32 g/cm^3.

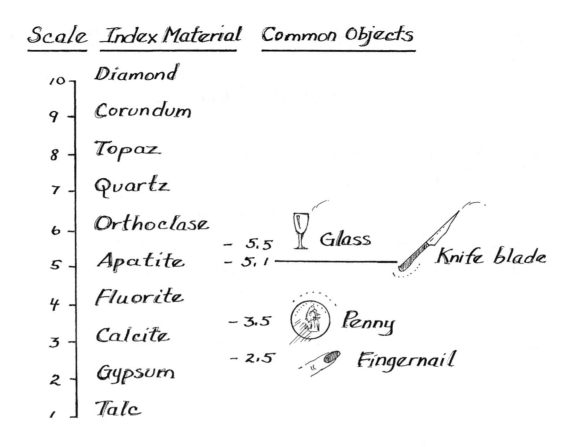

Scale	Index Material	Common Objects
10	Diamond	
9	Corundum	
8	Topaz	
7	Quartz	
6	Orthoclase	
		– 5.5 Glass
5	Apatite	– 5.1 ———————— Knife blade
4	Fluorite	
		– 3.5 Penny
3	Calcite	
		– 2.5 Fingernail
2	Gypsum	
1	Talc	

Hand out the Minerals Worksheet and proceed to work with small groups of students on some of the adaptations. Also, if time permits, have the students participate in the Whole Class Lab at the end of this activity.

Minerals Worksheet

1. Answer True or False to the following statements:

   a. _____ A mineral is an organic substance found in nature.

   b. _____ A common mineral formed from magma is iron.

   c. _____ Diamonds and rubies are not considered inorganic minerals.

   d. _____ Heat and pressure can change the composition of minerals.

   e. _____ The Mohs' scale is a scale to determine the luster of minerals.

2. List five characteristics of minerals:

   _____

   _____

   _____

   _____

   _____

3. In short-answer form, explain the four ways that minerals form.

   _____

   _____

   _____

4. List the seven ways that you can identify a mineral:

   _____   _____

   _____   _____

   _____   _____

   _____

How to Adapt This Lesson for the Inclusive Classroom

For Learning Disabled Students

Review the notes presented in class to reinforce the lesson. Give students partial notes to fill out during note taking (see page 98). True-or-false questions can be answered together in a group: first read each statement aloud and then ask students to find data that supports the answers in their notes.

Use the following mnemonic to aid students in remembering the seven ways that you can identify a mineral:

Competent Scientists Love Clapping Hands for Creative Discoveries

Competent = Color

Scientists = Streak

Love = Luster

Clapping = Crystal form

Hands = Hardness

For = Fracture

Creative = Cleavage

Discoveries = Density

For Resistant Learners or Students with ADD/ADHD

The mnemonic device above can be placed onto index cards, with one side stating the mineral property and the other the memory word. In pairs, students can quiz each other, placing the memory word face up and asking each other to identify the correct mineral property. This will help students focus while keeping the learning fast paced, interactive, and fun.

For Students with Fine Motor or Visual Difficulties

Because there are a lot of notes for this lesson, provide copies of the notes for these students. Also, have a scribe transfer completed answers to each student's worksheet. Finally, paraprofessionals can help students make study guides using unlined paper and colored markers. These study guides will list characteristics, formations, and properties of minerals.

For Gifted Learners

Expand on this lesson by having gifted learners make a mineral museum. Students can research at least ten minerals and find examples to bring into class. Display these minerals and information in the classroom for all to walk around, view, visit, and learn.

Whole Class Lab: Is It Really a Mineral?

Purpose: This lab will provide students with an opportunity to identify minerals in a group of items, based on what they have learned about minerals.

This lab works best with groups of four to five students.

Supplies (per group)

four magnifying glasses

four brown paper bags with the following items included in each:

    piece of rock salt

    penny

    small piece of iron ore

    nickel

    piece of granite or rock

    piece of quartz

    number 2 pencil

    piece of chalk

    tube of lip balm

    tube of sparkly eye shadow

    a nonmineral item such as a toy figurine or small car

piece of lined paper

pencil

1. Have students use their magnifying glasses to look carefully at all of the items in the bag. Using their notes from class pertaining to the characteristics of minerals, students should determine which items in the bag are minerals.

2. Have one student in each group write down the group's consensus and hand it in.

3   Discuss students' findings together as a class.

How to Adapt This Lab for the Inclusive Classroom

For Learning Disabled Students

Write down the characteristics of minerals on a sheet of paper to aid students' memory while they are investigating the items. Also consider making a chart and placing it on the whiteboard as a reference tool.

Home/School Connection

Give students the following assignment to complete at home:

> With your family, make a list of all of the common minerals that can be found around your house and their uses. Bring the list to class to discuss.

How to Evaluate This Lesson

Evaluate this lesson by assessing worksheets, class participation in the lab, and the completion of the Home/School Connection.

Activity 4: Oceans and Seas

Purpose: Students will learn to identify the four main oceans and note major differences between oceans and seas. They will also understand some features of the ocean floor.

Read through the lesson and the adaptations and make sure you have the supplies you will need.

Supplies for the main lesson

large map of the oceans, seas, and continents

chalkboard, overhead projector, computer with presentation software, or interactive whiteboard

copy of a drawing showing the main ocean features

science notebooks

Supplies for the adaptations

colored construction paper

index cards

pencils

diagram of a blank map

Lesson

1. Place the map of the ocean features in the front of the classroom where everyone can clearly see it.

2. Begin the lesson by saying something like, "Today we are going to talk about oceans and seas. Oceans cover at least 70 percent of the world. There are four main oceans."

3. Write the names of the oceans and the following information on the board, pointing to each ocean on the map as you describe it:

   a. **The Pacific Ocean:** The Pacific Ocean is the largest ocean on Earth. It is also the world's deepest ocean, at approximately 3,940 meters. The Pacific Ocean is located in the northern and southern hemispheres, west of North and South America.

   b. **The Atlantic Ocean:** The Atlantic Ocean, the second largest ocean, is approximately one half the size of the Pacific Ocean. It is more narrow and only about half as deep as the Pacific Ocean. The Atlantic Ocean is located in the northern and southern hemispheres, east of North and South America.

   c. **The Indian Ocean:** The Indian Ocean is only slightly smaller than the Atlantic Ocean and is about the same depth. The Indian Ocean is primarily located in the southern hemisphere, south of Asia.

   d. **The Arctic Ocean:** The Arctic Ocean is sometimes not defined as one of the world's main oceans because it is very small; it is only about 7 percent of the size of the Pacific Ocean and only about 25 percent as deep as the Atlantic Ocean. The Arctic Ocean goes around the North Pole.

4. Next, talk about the world's seas. Generate a discussion with the class by asking, "What is the main difference between an ocean and a sea?"

After prompting and brainstorming, lead the group to the following answer:

"The difference between an ocean and a sea is that most seas are defined by land masses. Water from the seas flows into one of the major world oceans. The term 'Seven Seas' has been used to loosely name the most common seas on the planet."

5. Write the names of the seven seas on the board and point to each on the map.
   a. Adriatic Sea
   b. Aegean Sea
   c. Arabian Sea
   d. Black Sea
   e. Caspian Sea
   f. Mediterranean Sea
   g. Red Sea

6. Explain why oceans and seas consist of salt water, saying, "Salt water comes from the seas that flow into the oceans, as well as undersea volcanic explosions that deposit minerals into the water. Salt also comes from water's washing over minerals and rocks for millions of years and depositing it into the oceans. This salt is the same salt that you use at the dinner table."

7. Describe the following features of the ocean floor and point to them on the drawing:
   a. **Continental Margin:** When walking along a shoreline, you are walking on the continental margin. The continental margin is the space between where the land ends and the basin floor begins. This area has very little volcanic activity, and is made of layers of undisturbed sediment or sand.

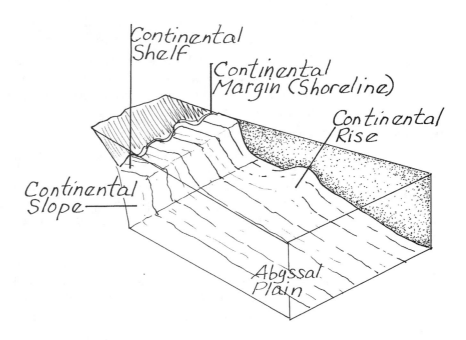

Differentiated Instruction for the Middle School Science Teacher

b. **Continental Shelf:** The continental shelf can extend as far as 1,500 kilometers from the shore. It usually is approximately 80 kilometers wide and 130 meters deep. The continental shelf contains important minerals, oil, and natural gas, as well as sand and gravel deposits.

c. **Continental Slope:** The continental slope is cut by deep canyons running perpendicular to the shoreline. The slope is much deeper than the shelf and serves as a boundary line between land and ocean.

d. **Continental Rise:** The continental rise is found between the continental slope and the abyssal plain. It is the last boundary between continents and represents the deepest part of the ocean. Oceanographers hope to study this area more to learn about the ocean and its geology.

e. **Abyssal Plain:** Abyssal plains are flat areas of the deep ocean floor.

Hand out the Oceans and Seas Worksheet and proceed to work with small groups of students on some of the adaptations. Also, if time permits, have the students participate in the Whole Class Lab at the end of this activity.

Oceans and Seas Worksheet

Match the following items.

1. _____ This ocean is the largest ocean on the planet.	a. Oceans
2. _____ This feature is found between the continental slope and the abyssal plain.	b. Indian Ocean
3. _____ This is the flat area of the ocean floor.	c. Continental Shelf
4. _____ This ocean is located mainly in the southern hemisphere of the world.	d. Abyssal Plain
5. _____ At least seven of these are defined and located by landmasses.	e. Pacific Ocean
6. _____ This ocean is one half the size of the Pacific Ocean.	f. Seas
7. _____ This is the scientific term for the coastline.	g. Atlantic Ocean
8. _____ This is an ocean feature that runs perpendicular to the shoreline.	h. Continental Slope
9. _____ This ocean is the smallest ocean on the planet.	i. Continental Rise
10. _____ Seventy percent of the world is covered by these.	j. Arctic Ocean

How to Adapt This Lesson for the Inclusive Classroom

For Learning Disabled Students

Using the notes presented in class, students can answer worksheet items in a small-group setting. One student can read an item aloud, while others peruse their notes and attempt to eliminate choices until they find the correct answer. They can also use sheets of construction paper to mask all other items.

Students may also use a blank world map, like the one on the next page, as a graphic organizer to label and remember seas and oceans.

For Resistant Learners or Students with ADD/ADHD

Students with behavioral difficulties may enjoy the interaction and fast-paced review of the game Name That Ocean, which requires two to four players.

Name That Ocean

1. Write each ocean name and ocean floor feature on one side of an index card.

2. Write three characteristics of each term on the opposite side of the card.

3. Divide students into two teams. Make labels for each team by folding two pieces of 8½- by 11-inch paper in half the long way and writing Team A and Team B on each side, respectively.

4. Shuffle the cards. Team A places a name card face up and asks Team B to define three characteristics of the term. Each characteristic is worth one point. Record the score.

5. Team B repeats the process. Additional rounds can be played showing the three characteristics face up and guessing the name of the ocean or ocean floor feature. The team with the most points wins.

For Gifted Learners

Expand on this lesson by asking students to make a topographical map of the ocean floor, which they then can label and present to the class.

Whole Class Lab: Sink or Swim?

Purpose: Students will see if a foil boat will stay afloat longer in salt or fresh water. In other words, they will learn which type of water is more buoyant.

This lab will work best with four students in each group.

Supplies (per group)

two 1-quart bowls

1 cup of salt

wooden spoon

two 12-inch pieces of aluminum foil

bag of marbles

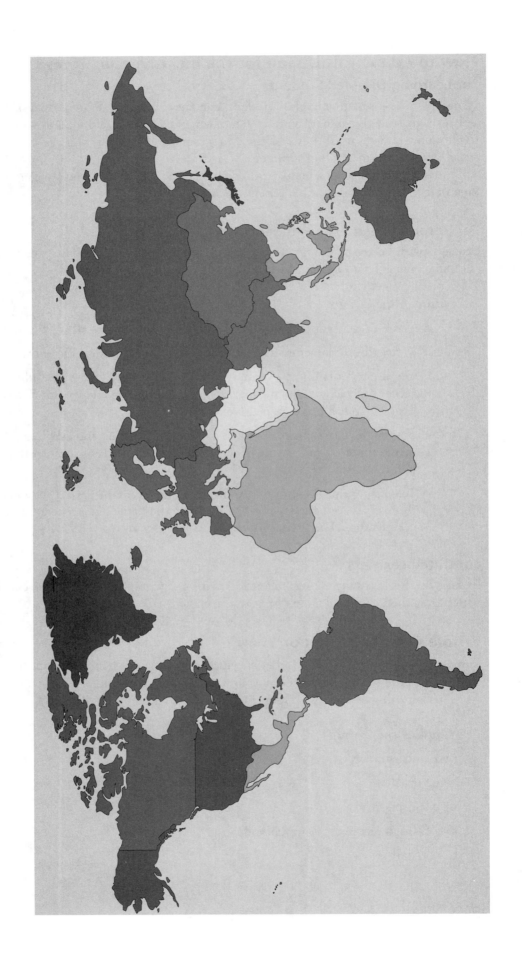

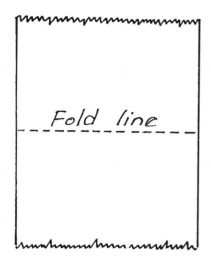

Fold line

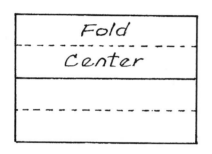

Fold Center

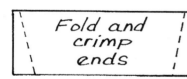

Fold and crimp ends

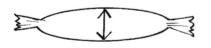

Spread to form canoe

1. Have each group fill their bowls with lukewarm water, pouring one cup of salt into one of the bowls and stirring to dissolve.

2. Students then fold their pieces of foil in half. Holding the foil lengthwise, they fold the bottom edge of each piece to its middle.

3. They then fold each piece of foil's top edge to the middle to meet the bottom fold, crimping the edges together to make a canoe.

4. Have each group place the boats in their two separate bowls, making sure these float.

5. Students place two marbles at a time in each boat, continuing the experiment until one of the boats sinks. Ask students to record their observations and hand in a conclusion about which type of water is more buoyant. Buoyancy refers to the force of an object being less than the fluid itself. This keeps an object afloat. The salt water should be more buoyant.

How to Adapt This Lab for the Inclusive Classroom

For Students with Fine Motor or Visual Difficulties

Ask these students to fill the bowls with water, add salt, and stir the mixtures. Avoid assigning them tasks that require a great deal of control, such as shaping the boats and adding the marbles.

For Students with Physical Disabilities

For wheelchair-bound students, make sure the bowls are placed at a level where all can participate and see the experiment as it progresses.

Home/School Connection

Give students the following assignment to complete at home:

Research different resources that can be obtained from the ocean floor. Write a one-page essay explaining two resources and their everyday uses. Also, think about how these resources might be used in the future. Bring your essay to class to hand in.

How to Evaluate This Lesson

Evaluate this lesson in two parts.

Part One (70 percent): Use the worksheet, class participation, and lab to assess students' knowledge of oceans and seas.

Part Two (30 percent): Interview each student about the research he or she completed at home, asking the following questions:

What were the two resources you researched?

How do they benefit the world now, and how might they do so in the future?

Activity 5: The Solar System

Purpose: Students will understand and identify features of the sun and the planets in the solar system.

Read through the lesson and the adaptations and make sure you have the supplies you will need.

Supplies for the main lesson:

chart of the solar system

chalkboard, overhead projector, computer with presentation software, or interactive whiteboard

science notebooks

Internet access

Supplies for the adaptations:

assorted colored highlighters

index cards

colored construction paper

poster board

Lesson

1. Display the chart of the solar system at the front of the class where everyone can see it.

2. Begin the lesson by saying something like, "Today we are going to learn about the sun and our solar system. We will define all of the planets and other objects that revolve around the sun. What can you tell me about the solar system?" Lead a discussion to discover what the students already know.

3. When there has been enough discussion, continue, "Currently, scientists believe that there are eight planets that revolve around the sun. They are Mercury, Venus, Earth, Mars, Jupiter, Saturn, Uranus, and Neptune. Pluto, once considered the ninth planet, has been renamed as a minor or dwarf planet, although not every scientist agrees with this designation. In addition to the planets, the other objects in the solar system include the sun, the moons that orbit the planets, and asteroids."

4. Write the names of the objects in the solar system on the board and have students copy the information down in their notebooks:

    a. **The Sun:** The sun is Earth's primary source of energy and life. It is classified as a yellow star, which burns at a moderate heat for a star.

    b. **Mercury:** The planet Mercury is named after a Roman god. It is the second smallest planet and the planet closest to the sun. Mercury has no moons. It orbits the sun faster than any other planet known, taking eighty-eight Earth days to complete one orbit around the sun. Mercury is very dry and extremely hot. It is a terrestrial planet, as are Venus, Earth, and Mars, meaning it is made up primarily of metal and rock. These planets are known as the inner planets, because they are relatively close to the sun. Plants and animals could not survive on Mercury due to its extreme heat, lack of oxygen, and very thin atmosphere.

c. **Venus:** The planet Venus is named after the Roman goddess of love and beauty. Venus is a beautiful planet to observe. Its surface is rocky and dusty, and contains lava, mountains, canyons, and plains. There is no water or oxygen on Venus, so life as we know it cannot exist on this planet. Its atmosphere is made of carbon dioxide, nitrogen, and sulfuric acid. It takes 225 Earth days for Venus to orbit the sun.

d. **Earth:** Earth is the third planet from the sun and the fifth largest planet in our solar system. The name "Earth" comes from Old English and German languages. Over 70 percent of our Earth is covered with water. The atmosphere contains mainly nitrogen and oxygen. With the heat of the sun, this atmospheric composition makes living conditions optimal for plant and animal life. It takes Earth 365 days, or one year, to orbit the sun. Earth has one moon.

e. **Mars:** The planet Mars is red and named after the ancient Roman god of war. Mars can be seen in detail from Earth. Mars has two moons, called Phobos and Deimos. The atmosphere of Mars is mostly carbon dioxide. This planet has been explored since the 1960s. To date, no evidence of life as we know it has been discovered on Mars. The temperature of Mars goes from –220 to 60 degrees Fahrenheit, which means that Mars gets extremely cold. It takes approximately two Earth years for Mars to orbit the sun.

f. **Asteroid Belt:** The asteroid belt is located between Mars and Jupiter. It separates the inner planets of Mercury, Venus, Earth, and Mars from the outer planets, Saturn, Jupiter, Uranus, and Neptune. Scientists believe the irregular pieces of debris, or asteroids, that are found orbiting the sun in this region of the solar system are planets that never formed. The asteroids are made up primarily of nickel and iron.

g. **Jupiter:** Jupiter is the Roman name for the Greek god Zeus. It is the largest planet in our solar system. Jupiter has sixty-three moons. The most well-known moons of Jupiter are Europa, Callisto, and Ganymede. It takes twelve Earth years for Jupiter to orbit the sun. Jupiter is very gaseous. It makes up one of the five gaseous planets in the solar system, the others being Saturn, Uranus, Neptune, and Pluto. Jupiter does not have a solid surface. The gaseous composition is 90 percent hydrogen and 10 percent helium. Therefore, life as we know it could not exist on Jupiter. Jupiter is noted for its "Great Red Spot," which is visible through a telescope. This identifying feature has been explained as a high-pressure region that stands out as being much higher and colder than the surrounding atmospheric regions.

h. **Saturn:** The planet Saturn is named after the Roman god Saturnus. It is the second largest planet, has at least thirty-one moons, and is known for its beautiful rings. The surface of Saturn is liquid and gas, with an atmosphere of both hydrogen and helium. Therefore, no known life can exist on Saturn.

Saturn's temperature is approximately –288 degrees Fahrenheit, which is extremely cold. It takes Saturn approximately thirty Earth years to orbit the sun.

i. **Uranus:** The planet Uranus is named after the Greek god of the sky. It is the third largest planet in the solar system. Uranus's atmosphere is made up mostly of hydrogen. Helium and methane gases make up another 20 percent of the atmosphere. Life as we know it cannot exist in these conditions. Uranus has at least twenty-seven moons. Occasionally it can be seen without a telescope. It takes Uranus approximately eighty-four Earth years to orbit the sun. This planet is very cold, with temperatures of about –323 degrees Fahrenheit.

j. **Neptune:** Neptune is the eighth planet from the sun, and is also known as the "Blue Giant." It is the outermost gaseous planet, comprised of mostly hydrogen. Helium and methane make up approximately 26 percent of the remaining gases. Therefore, no known life forms can exist on this planet. Neptune has eight known moons. One moon, Triton, is known to have the coldest temperature in our solar system at negative 391 degrees Fahrenheit. It takes Neptune approximately 165 Earth years to orbit the sun.

k. **Pluto:** Pluto was discovered in 1930 by Clyde Tombaugh, and is named after the Greek god of the Underworld. Originally considered a planet, Pluto is now generally thought of as within a separate category of dwarf planet. Pluto has not been explored via satellite. It has at least one moon, Charon. Pluto's surface is made up of nitrogen, carbon monoxide, methane gas, and water ice. No life forms as we know them can exist in this climate. It takes approximately 248 Earth years for Pluto to orbit the sun.

Hand out the Solar System Worksheet and proceed to work with small groups of students on some of the adaptations. Also, if time permits, have the students participate in the Whole Class Lab at the end of this activity.

Solar System Worksheet

Circle the best possible answer for each question.

1. The smallest terrestrial planet that has no moons is called:
   a. Venus
   b. Neptune
   c. Mercury
   d. Charon

2. The planet that takes 365 days to orbit the sun is called:
   a. Jupiter
   b. Earth
   c. Mars
   d. Venus

3. The planet Earth's primary source of energy is:
   a. the moon
   b. Phobos
   c. the sun
   d. Deimos

4. A planet that can get as cold as −220 degrees Fahrenheit and is red is:
   a. Jupiter
   b. Saturn
   c. Mars
   d. Uranus

5. Asteroids are pieces of nickel and iron that:
   a. warm the earth
   b. separate the inner and outer planets
   c. rotate around the moon
   d. form into stars, creating a belt

6. The Great Red Spot has been identified as a high-pressure spot on the planet:
   a. Saturn
   b. Neptune
   c. Uranus
   d. Jupiter

7. The second largest planet in our solar system is:
   a. Earth
   b. Neptune
   c. Saturn
   d. Jupiter

8. Uranus's atmosphere is made up of:
   a. nitrogen, oxygen, and water
   b. oxygen, hydrogen, and ice
   c. nitrogen, carbon monoxide, and ice
   d. hydrogen, helium, and methane

9. The planet Earth is composed of:
   a. approximately 70 percent water
   b. approximately 70 percent land
   c. approximately 70 percent lava
   d. all of the above

10. Pluto's moon is called:
    a. Charon
    b. Triton
    c. Europa
    d. Orion

How to Adapt This Lesson for the Inclusive Classroom

For Learning Disabled Students

Review the notes presented in class with these students, having them use a graphic organizer to write down the main highlights of each planet. Students who have difficulty memorizing the order of the planets in relation to the sun can create a mnemonic, such as the following:

My Very Educated Mom Just Served Us Nachos

My	= Mercury
Very	= Venus
Educated	= Earth
Mom	= Mars
Just	= Jupiter
Served	= Saturn
Us	= Uranus
Nachos	= Neptune

When students are answering multiple choice questions, model a self-talk strategy (see example below) to help them find the correct answer. Students will then repeat the strategy for the remaining items.

Talking to Myself About the Solar System

The teacher will first read the script to the students, and then students will read the script alone:

"Let's take a look at the first multiple choice question. I will read it out loud. It says:

1. The smallest terrestrial planet that has no moons is called:

    a. Venus

    b. Neptune

    c. Mercury

    d. Charon

"Let's see. I should probably look at the question to see if there are any identifying words that could give me a clue as to what planet group I should look at. I will underline those words. I see two clue words already. One is the word 'smallest.' I am supposed to look for the smallest planet. The other word is 'terrestrial.' I remember the teacher saying that the terrestrial planets are Mercury, Venus, Earth, and Mars. That means that the answer is probably one of these four planets.

"Those seem like pretty good clues to me. Let's look at my answer choices. We have Venus, Neptune, Mercury, and Charon. Right away I know that Neptune can't be a possibility, because Neptune is not a terrestrial planet.

"Let me think about Charon. Is that a planet? Let me view my note cards for factoids. Do I have a card on Charon? No. I should probably look at the moon names then. I'll look through all of my factoid cards until I see some names of moons. Okay, we have Triton, and Europa, and . . . there it is . . . Charon. . . . Charon is Pluto's moon."

"That leaves only Venus and Mercury for answer choices. Let me look at my clue words again. I remember that one key clue word was 'smallest.' I have it underlined. I know that Mercury is smaller than Venus, based on the information we got from the teacher in class. Therefore, the correct answer is 'c.' Mercury!"

For Students with Visual Difficulties

Students can use colored bookmarks, made from construction paper, to cover other answer choices when answering the multiple choice questions. This will minimize extraneous text.

For Resistant Learners or Students with ADD/ADHD

The interactive game below can be used as a whole class activity or can be done in small groups of students who have attentional concerns.

Whose Planet Is It Anyway?

1. Using index cards, have students write down as many facts about each planet as possible that were covered in class. Encourage students to use class notes. Have extra note cards available for the game.

2. Make the cards into a deck and shuffle.

3. Have one student pick a card. He or she can then begin acting out the main features of the planet, much like in the game Charades. Hand blank cards to the students who are watching and have them quietly guess what planet is being mimicked. The student with the correct answer will receive a point. The student who guesses correctly will take the next turn. Continue the game until all the planets are guessed. The student with the highest score wins the game.

For Gifted Learners

Have students design and construct three-dimensional models of a chosen planet, including facts other than those covered in class. Students may use the Internet and books for research. Have them put their additional factoids on posters and present their projects to the class.

Whole Class Lab: Use the Power of the Sun to Make a Solar Stove

Purpose: This lab will illustrate how the sun's energy can heat water as students create a solar cooker.

This experiment works best with groups of three or four students.

Supplies (per group)

empty 1-pound coffee can

drill (not for student use)

18-inch piece of yarn or rope

black craft paint

paint brush

8- by 10-inch piece of Styrofoam

two 6- by 8-inch mirrors (purchased at a pharmacy or dollar store)

5- by 7-inch mirror

teacup

tea bag

bottle of water

thermometer

oven mitt

Top View

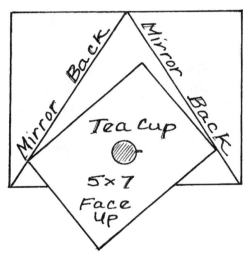

Front View with Coffee Can On

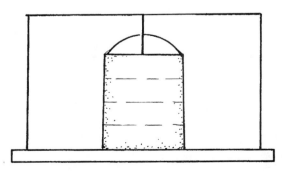

1. Drill two holes in the bottom of each group's coffee can. Each group then takes the piece of yarn or rope, threads it through the holes, and ties a knot on the inside, forming a handle.

2. Have students paint their coffee cans black and set them aside to dry.

3. Students then press the two larger mirrors into the Styrofoam block so they touch each other in the center, forming a triangle. Make sure the reflective sides are facing in. The smaller mirror will simply sit face up on top of the Styrofoam.

4. Have students bring their coffee cans and the Styrofoam blocks with mirrors outside on a sunny day. Students then fill their teacups ¾ of the way with tap or bottled water. Next, each group places their teacup on top of the smaller mirror.

5. Have students take the temperature of the water using thermometers and record this information on paper.

6. Have each group place the tea bag in the water, cover the mirrors with the coffee can, and allow the cup to sit in the solar stove for two hours.

7. Students should use oven mitts to carefully pull each coffee can off the stove by its string.

8. Have students take the temperature of the water again to determine and record what changed in regard to the temperature and look of the water.

9. Students can go online to research what other recipes might work in a solar stove, exploring, for example, how these stoves might be used for camping. Groups should write their results together and hand them in at the end of the lab.

How to Adapt This Lab for the Inclusive Classroom
For Students with Physical Disabilities or Visual Difficulties
Make sure someone who is used to working the stove removes the coffee can lid and takes the water temperature the second time.

Home/School Connection
Give students the following assignment to complete at home:

> Interview family members, asking them the questions, "Do you think there is life on other planets? Why or why not?" Compare and contrast these results with the notes presented in class. What are your thoughts? Write an essay of about 250 words answering these questions, and bring it to class.

How to Evaluate This Lesson
Evaluate this lesson using the Home/School Connection, lab results, and worksheets to determine students' mastery of the concepts presented in the lesson. You may want to use the following rubric:

Conceptual understanding (50 percent): Grade the essay written for homework based on how well students incorporate knowledge of the solar system presented in class while simultaneously evaluating others' opinions about life on other planets.

Concrete understanding (25 percent): Grade the worksheet to determine students' mastery of information about the solar system.

Class participation (25 percent): For this category, assess students' lab performance and written lab results.

Activity 6: Stars and Galaxies

Purpose: Students will be able to name and identify a variety of stars and galaxies based on specific characteristics.

Read through the lesson and the adaptations and make sure you have the supplies you will need.

Supplies for the main lesson

chalkboard, overhead projector, computer with presentation software, or interactive whiteboard

science notebooks

Supplies for the adaptations

flip chart

assorted wide, colored markers

Lite-Brite

tabletop bell

poster board

Lesson

1. Begin the lesson by saying something like, "Today we are going to learn about stars and galaxies and their defining features."

2. Begin by describing stars, saying, "Stars light and heat our planet. They can be old or young. At first glance, all stars appear to be white. But upon further investigation with a telescope, you can see that stars vary in color. The variations in color depend on the heat of the stars."

3. Write the following descriptions on the board and have students copy them down in their notebooks:

   a. **Red Stars:** Red stars are cooler stars. They have longer wavelengths of heat and emit red light. They range in temperature from 2,000 to 3,500 degrees Kelvin. Kelvin, like Celsius, is an absolute temperature scale.

   b. **Blue Stars:** Blue stars are very hot stars. Their wavelengths are very short and they have surface temperatures of almost 30,000 degrees Kelvin.

   c. **White Stars:** White stars are hot stars. One white star, Vega, is the star to which astronomers calibrate all other stars in terms of color. This star is approximately fifty-four times brighter than the sun, and has a temperature of approximately 9,300 degrees Kelvin.

   d. **Yellow Stars:** Yellow stars emit wavelengths of medium length and have moderate temperatures. Their range of heat is between 5,000 and 6,000 degrees Kelvin. An example of a yellow star is the sun.

   e. **Interstellar Matter:** The space between stars contains clouds of dust and gases, which are referred to as interstellar matter. When this matter is very close to a hot star, it will glow.

f. **Nuclear Fusion:** Stars exist because of a process called nuclear fusion, by which multiple like-charged atomic nuclei join together to form a heavier nucleus. It releases an enormous amount of energy, which we see as light and feel as heat. Scientists are working on ways to recreate nuclear fusion in power plants. Currently, nuclear power plants use nuclear fission, in which atoms are split to release energy.

g. **Light-Years:** A light-year is a measure of the distance light travels in one year. Light travels about 1,800,000 kilometers in a minute, or approximately 10 trillion kilometers per year. Light-years are used to describe the large distances to stars.

4. Continue by describing galaxies, saying, "Galaxies are large clusters of stars that are many light-years across. Within each galaxy, there are several trillion stars. There are four main types of galaxies. These are spiral, elliptical, lenticular, and irregular galaxies." Write the following definitions on the board and have students copy them down in their notebooks:

a. **Spiral Galaxies:** A spiral galaxy has a core center or disk that is round and flat. The disk burns very hot and includes interstellar matter. All around the center are spiral patterns of stars in a cluster, resembling tails. The Milky Way is an example of a spiral galaxy.

b. **Elliptical Galaxies:** Elliptical galaxies have no core center or disc. They are an elliptical shape and appear to be large, spiral patterns of stars. The nearest elliptical galaxy to the Milky Way is the Andromeda galaxy.

c. **Lenticular Galaxies:** Lenticular galaxies are short spiral galaxies that resemble disks but do not burn hot. They lack the star mass and spiral patterns that are seen in a spiral galaxy. The nearest lenticular galaxy to the Milky Way is called the Canis Major Dwarf galaxy.

d. **Irregular Galaxies:** Irregular galaxies have different shapes. The most familiar irregular galaxies are the Large and Small Megellanic Clouds, which are both visible without a telescope.

5. Explain that galaxies are also distinguished by the age of the stars within them: "Galaxies with young stars burn very hot. Irregular galaxies contain young stars. Elliptical and lenticular galaxies contain mostly older stars, which are not as hot. The Milky Way is a combination of old and young stars."

Hand out the Stars and Galaxies Worksheet and proceed to work with small groups of students on some of the adaptations. Also, if time permits, have the students participate in the Whole Class Lab at the end of this activity.

Name: _____   Date: _____

Stars and Galaxies Worksheet

Answer the following questions by filling in the blank spaces.

1. A star that is considered cool is a _____ star.

2. A _____ measures the distance light travels in one year.

3. The process that keeps stars burning is called: _____.

4. The _____ burns between 5,000 and 6,000 degrees Kelvin.

5. A white star that astronomers use as a standard to measure against other stars
    is called: _____.

6. The Milky Way is a _____ galaxy.

7. The spaces between stars filled with clouds and dust are called: _____.

8. Short spiral galaxies that resemble disks but do not burn hot are called: _____.

9. An example of an elliptical galaxy is the: _____.

10. Large clusters of stars are called: _____.

How to Adapt This Lesson for the Inclusive Classroom
For Learning Disabled Students

Review the notes aloud with a small group of students. Students can take notes using a partial notes graphic organizer (see page 98). A word bank will also aid students who have difficulty remembering the content of the notes. Place these words on a flip chart or piece of poster board and have students check off words once they've been used on the worksheet.

interstellar matter	spiral
red	galaxies
light-year	sun
Andromeda galaxy	lenticular galaxies
Vega	nuclear fusion

For Students with Visual Difficulties

Students can write their answers to the worksheet on a separate piece of paper using a larger space. Write words on a flip chart with thick markers to make viewing easier. Lastly, use a Lite-Brite to provide a visual example of galaxies and different colored stars.

For Resistant Learners or Students with ADD/ADHD

These students benefit greatly from interactive learning. Using the worksheet sentences and word bank listed above, play the following interactive game, designed for four players:

Let the Force Be with You

1. In the first round, have one student read each worksheet question out loud.

2. Place a small tabletop bell in the middle of three students. Once the question is read, the first student to ring the bell gets to answer the question. If correct, that student receives one point. If the answer is incorrect, the next student is asked to answer the item. The game continues until all questions have been asked and answered correctly.

3. In the second round, state a word bank word and ask students to define it. Again, the student who rings the bell first and gets the answer right receives a point. The highest-scoring student obtains the "Force."

4. The game may be repeated until all students have mastered the items. Students then fill out worksheet questions.

For Gifted Learners

Expand on this lesson by having gifted students develop and present a PowerPoint presentation on galaxies, showing types of galaxies and explaining interesting facts about the varieties covered in class.

Whole Class Lab: Stargazing

Purpose: Students will identify various constellations.

This experiment works best with groups of four students.

Supplies

graph paper

pencils

blank transparencies

permanent markers

overhead projector

masking tape

1. Assign each group two constellations, out of the following possibilities:

    Big Dipper

    Orion

    Pegasus

    Hercules

    Ursa Minor

    Ursa Major

    Little Dipper

    Phoenix

    Cassiopeia

2. Students then research the assigned constellations.

3. Have groups plot the constellations on graph paper.

4. Each group then draws the constellations on transparencies with a permanent marker.

5. Place the transparencies on the overhead projector, turn out the lights, and project the constellations on the wall. Using masking tape, students can then mark the outlines of the constellations on the walls.

How to Adapt This Lab for the Inclusive Classroom
For Students with Physical Disabilities

Outlining constellations on the wall or board with masking tape may be a difficult undertaking for these students. Give students plenty of responsibility during the early steps of this lab, when the workload is less physically demanding.

Home/School Connection

Give students the following assignment to complete at home:

Research your zodiac or birthdate sign and its associated constellation. Make a model and bring in information regarding your constellation to present orally to the class.

How to Evaluate This Lesson

Assess students' individual presentations of the Home/School Connection, in which they should review all information regarding constellations and zodiac signs. The presentation should last approximately five minutes, and be graded on content, delivery, and visual aids.

Activity 7: The Water Cycle

Purpose: Students will be able to identify and understand all of the components of the water cycle.

Read through the lesson and the adaptations and make sure you have the supplies you will need.

Supplies for the main lesson

chalkboard, overhead projector, computer with presentation software, or interactive whiteboard

science notebooks

Supplies for the adaptations

lined paper

colored markers or pencils

construction paper

index cards

string

beads—light blue, brown, blue, green, yellow, clear (one each), two white beads

Lesson

1. Begin the lesson by saying something like, "Today we are going to learn about the water cycle and how you can use it to predict the weather. Does anyone know what the water cycle is?" Use this question to begin a discussion about the water cycle.

2. Explain that water has three forms, all of which are included in the water cycle, and write the forms on the board.

   a. Solid (ice)

   b. Liquid (water)

   c. Gas (water vapor)

3. Explain the water cycle by saying something like, "Water moves on Earth in a continuous loop or cycle. It is constantly changing its form between a solid, liquid, and gas. The water in the oceans is heated up by the sun. The heated water evaporates into the atmosphere.

   "This air now contains moisture from the water. The winds blow this moisture-filled air, and it condenses into water and ice crystals, forming clouds. The clouds become filled with moisture, and water, in the form of rain or snow, falls to the earth. The water then sinks into the ground, helping the soil and vegetation. All excess goes back into the lakes, streams, and oceans. Then the cycle repeats itself."

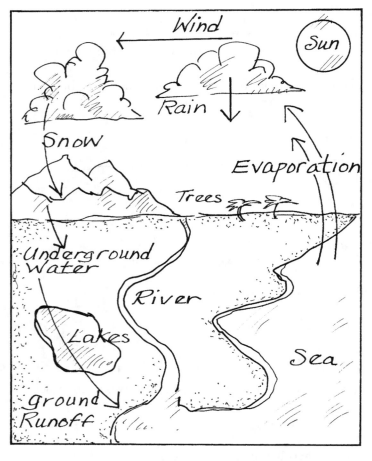

4. Write the following definitions of some common terms related to the water cycle on the board and have students copy them down in their notebooks:

a. **Evaporation:** This is the process by which a liquid becomes a vapor or gas. The sun heats up the water on the surface of oceans, lakes, rivers, and other bodies of water, which causes the water to evaporate and the vapor to rise into the atmosphere.

b. **Condensation:** This is the process by which a gas becomes a liquid. Winds allow evaporated water vapor to rise in the atmosphere. As it gets higher, it gets colder and turns back into little drops of water and ice that form clouds.

c. **Precipitation:** Precipitation occurs when the clouds become saturated with moisture from water and ice crystals. The excess liquid falls to Earth in the form of rain, freezing rain, snow, ice, or hail.

d. **Percolation:** This is the movement of water through rocks and soil. Much of the water that falls on the ground ends up back in the lakes, rivers, and streams through the process of percolation.

e. **Transpiration:** This is the process through which water evaporates from plants.

Hand out the Water Cycle Worksheet and proceed to work with small groups of students on some of the adaptations. Also, if time permits, have the students participate in the Whole Class Lab at the end of this activity.

Name: _____   Date: _____

Water Cycle Worksheet

Answer the following questions on the lines provided.

1. Identify the three forms of water and give an example of each.

   _____

   _____

   _____

2. Define the following terms:

   a. Percolation:

   _____

   _____

   _____

   b. Condensation:

   _____

   _____

   _____

   c. Precipitation:

   _____

   _____

   _____

   d. Transpiration:

   _____

   _____

   _____

3. In your own words, briefly explain the water cycle or draw a diagram that illustrates it.

   _____

   _____

   _____

How to Adapt This Lesson for the Inclusive Classroom

For Learning Disabled Students

Read the class notes on the water cycle aloud. Ask students to paraphrase each step. Coach the students to explain each step with the fewest possible words. Fold pieces of lined paper into quarters and hand these out to the students. Have students write each step of the water cycle in separate columns on their papers. Each step can be written with a different colored pencil or marker. Once students understand the concepts, these answers can be transferred to the worksheets. Students who have difficulty memorizing information can use some sort of memory clue, such as a song or a water cycle bracelet with each step represented by a different colored bead. For example:

White bead	= condensation (cloud)
Light blue bead	= precipitation (rain)
Brown bead	= accumulation (groundwater)
Blue bead	= surface runoff (water in lakes, river, ocean)
Green bead	= transpiration (water from plants)
Yellow bead	= sun (source of energy that keeps cycle moving)
Clear bead	= evaporation (water vapor)
White bead	= cloud (back to condensation)

Beads could be threaded on a string and tied to make a bracelet.

For Students with Fine Motor, Visual, or Perceptual Difficulties

Students can complete answers to the worksheet on the computer using a larger font. Also, in order to reduce the amount of writing, paraprofessionals could draw the cycle and students can label the steps of the water cycle.

For Gifted Learners

Expand on this lesson by having students research various types of clouds and their impacts on the weather. Encourage students to find pictures of cloud types and include them in their reports. Have students present their findings to the class.

Whole Class Lab: When It Rains It Pours

Purpose: Students will create their own water cycle and witness the steps in action.
  This experiment works best if every student works individually or with a partner.

Supplies (per student or pair of students)

1-quart clear plastic jar with a hole drilled in the lid

strip of adhesive tape

½ to 1 cup of potting soil, moistened thoroughly with water

½ cup of grass clippings, weeds, or small stones

ice pack or small zipper-lock bag filled with ice cubes

1. Have each student or pair cover the hole in the lid of the jar with the adhesive tape strip.

2. Students then pat moistened potting soil into the lids of their jars, topping these with grass clippings and sprinkling with additional water. Ask students to screw the jars on the lids so that they are standing upside down.

3. Have students place their jars in the sun for two hours. The insides of the jars should fill with steam.

4. Each student or pair then places the ice pack or bag of ice on the top of the jar and watches what happens.

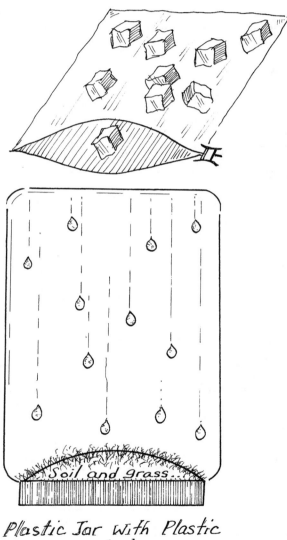

Plastic Jar with Plastic Lid

5. Once the experiment is completed, each student should explain the components of the water cycle on a sheet of paper and turn it in.

Explain how the following components of the water cycle are seen in this experiment. Hand in your findings.

a. Evaporation:

_____

_____

_____

_____

_____

_____

b. Condensation:

_____

_____

_____

_____

_____

_____

c. Precipitation:

_____

_____

_____

_____

_____

_____

d. Percolation:

_____

_____

_____

_____

_____

_____

How to Adapt This Lab for the Inclusive Classroom

For Learning Disabled Students

In a small group, review class notes and discuss how these pertain to the experiment before students complete the lab questions. Students can also draw diagrams of what they see during the experiment and label them with the key components of the water cycle.

For Resistant Learners or Students with ADD/ADHD

Allow students who are easily distracted to work with a partner for this experiment.

Home/School Connection

Give students the following assignment to complete at home:

> Over the course of one week, observe the clouds in the sky three times with your family. Take a survey, asking each family member to describe the clouds and record their responses on a sheet of paper. Take note of the weather on those days and record. Bring your data to class for a discussion.

How to Evaluate This Lesson

We recommend using a student-teacher interview format to assess students' mastery of this lesson. Ask students individually to explain the water cycle in their own words.

Chapter 7

Life
Science

Activity 1: Classification of Organisms

Purpose: Students will learn about the classification system and why scientists classify organisms.

Read through the lesson and the adaptations and make sure you have the supplies you will need.

Supplies for the main lesson

chalkboard, overhead projector, computer with presentation software, or interactive whiteboard

small jar of assorted change

science notebooks

Internet access

Supplies for the adaptations

index cards

assorted colored highlighters

poster board

white lined paper

stopwatch

Internet access

Lesson

1. Begin by saying something like, "Today we are going to learn about the classification system and why scientists classify organisms. Before we do that, however, let's explore the reasons why it is important to have a system of classification." Ask for two volunteers.

2. Give each student a handful of assorted change and ask the students to quickly calculate how much change is in front of them.

3. Now say, "I will ask each of you to organize the change in the most effective way you can." Once the money is organized, ask the students how much change they have in front of them. Note the difference in the time it took students to count the change before and after it was organized.

4. Begin a discussion with the class, having students answer the following questions:

   a. What did you observe that was different about counting the money the second time?

   b. Why is the money easier to count after it is organized?

   c. How might organizing organisms be helpful to scientists?

   Lead the students to the answer that classifying organisms, similar to organizing the loose change, makes it easier for scientists to study them.

5. Explain the classification system that scientists currently use, noting that there are eight classification levels that scientists use for organisms. Write the names on the board in order from highest to lowest: domain, kingdom, phylum, class, order, family, genus, and species.

Then say, "The domain is the highest level in the system, and the species the lowest. For example, a cat belongs to the domain Eukarya, the kingdom Animalia, the phylum Chordata, the class Mammalia, the order Carnivora, the family Felidae, the genus Felis, and the species Domestica."

Classification of a House Cat

Domain	Eukarya (cells with nuclei)
Kingdom	Animalia (are multicellular and are heterotrophs; rely directly or indirectly on other organisms for their nourishment)
Phylum	Chordata (have a backbone)
Class	Mammalia (animals that have fur and breast-feed young)
Order	Carnivora (meat-eating animals)
Family	Felidae (cats)
Genus	Felis (cats)
Species	Domestica (domesticated animals)

6. Explain that organisms are placed into domains and kingdoms based on their cell type, the number of cells in their bodies, and their ability to make food for themselves. Write the following information about the three main domains on the board for students to copy down in their notebooks:

   a. **Bacteria:** Members of the domain Bacteria have cells that do not have a nuclei. Bacteria are very common. You can find them on all things you touch and in the foods you eat. Yogurt is filled with good bacteria. Some bacteria are beneficial to the human body, and others can make you ill.

   b. **Archaea:** Members of the domain Archaea are found in harsh environments, such as hot springs, swamps, ocean floors, salt water, and animal intestines. They are different from bacteria, but also contain cells that have no nuclei.

   c. **Eukarya:** Members of the domain Eukarya are divided into four kingdoms: protists, plants, animals, and fungi. All cells in the animals of the domain Eukarya contain nuclei.

7. Then define and give examples from the four kingdoms of the domain Eukarya.

   a. **Protists:** Protists are organisms that are very different from any other. They do not neatly fit into any one category, but contain nuclei. An example of a protist is seaweed.

b. **Fungi:** Fungi are organisms that mostly feed by absorbing nutrients from other organisms. Examples of fungi are mushrooms, mold, mildew, and yeast.

c. **Plants:** Plants make their own food and include a wide variety of organisms. Flowering plants, vegetables, weeds, and trees are all included in this kingdom.

d. **Animals:** All land, air, and sea animals are part of the domain Eukarya.

Hand out the Classification of Organisms Worksheet and proceed to work with small groups of students on some of the adaptations. Also, if time permits, have the students participate in the Whole Class Lab at the end of this activity.

Name: _____   Date: _____

Classification of Organisms Worksheet

Fill in the answers to the following questions.

1. The three main domains that scientists use to classify organisms are:

    _____

    _____

    _____

2. The four kingdoms in the Eukarya domain are:

    _____

    _____

    _____

    _____

3. Give an example of an organism in each kingdom found in the domain Eukarya:

    Protists: _____

    Fungi: _____

    Plants: _____

    Animals: _____

4. The eight classification levels used by scientists to study organisms (in order from highest to lowest) are:

    _____

    _____

    _____

    _____

    _____

    _____

    _____

    _____

5. Using the scientific classification system and the Internet or a reference book, fill in the chart showing the names of all levels for classifying the organism "dog."

Classification of a Dog

How to Adapt This Lesson for the Inclusive Classroom
For Learning Disabled Students

Review the notes and terms aloud with a small group of students. With different high-lighters, write the three domains and the four main kingdoms in the domain Eukarya on one side of the index cards. Include examples of each on the other side of the index cards, and use the cards for a memory game or a review. Have students work in small groups and quiz one another until they master the concept of the classification system.

To remember the classification levels, have students try this mnemonic:

Dirty Kitchens Prevent Chefs' Omelets from Getting Sold

Dirty	= Domain
Kitchens	= Kingdom
Prevent	= Phylum
Chefs'	= Class
Omelets	= Order
From	= Family
Getting	= Genus
Sold	= Species

For Students with Visual Difficulties

Use poster board to make a large graphic organizer. Draw a pyramid on the poster board depicting the eight classification levels. This will visually arrange the information and make viewing easier for these students.

Domain

Kingdom

Phylum

Class

Order

Family

Genus

Species

Once students understand classification levels, they can play the following game, for four to eight players, which involves organizing animals, plants, and bacteria using this system:

Classification Craze

1. Write the names of animals, plants, or bacteria on the index cards and place them face down in a pile.

2. Students will form two teams.

3. Each group picks a card. Students have five minutes to fill in a classification chart, using a piece of lined paper folded in half. Students will list the classification level on one side and the corresponding answer for the organism on the other for the

item on their chosen card. They may use the Internet or notes presented in class. Assist each group using the Internet to find the answers.

4. The group that first completes their chart accurately receives a point, and each team picks another card.

5. The team with the most points is the winner.

For Resistant Learners or Students with ADD/ADHD

To engage students with behavioral difficulties, include them in the Classification Craze game, as it is interactive and structured.

For Gifted Learners

Expand on this lesson by having gifted students design a board game involving the classification of organisms. When finished, students can demonstrate the game to the class.

Whole Class Lab: Make Your Own Yogurt

Purpose: Students will learn about healthy bacterial fermentation and reproduction, having just learned about the classification of plants and bacteria.

This lab works best with groups of three or four students working with you, an aide, or a parent volunteer at a stove in a cafeteria or life skills room.

Supplies (per group)

copy of recipe in large font

2 cups of milk

2 tablespoons of active live culture yogurt (vanilla)

2 tablespoons of honey

sterilized 16-ounce glass jar with a lid

candy thermometer

2-quart saucepan

large thermos with a lid, wide enough to fit the jar inside

wooden spoon

1. With their adult supervisor, have each group heat the milk in the saucepan until it reaches 180 degrees Fahrenheit, and then turn off the burner.

2. Have each group add the yogurt and honey to the hot milk, mixing for one minute with wooden spoons.

3. Students then transfer the mixture into their jars. Each group tightens the lid and places the jar into their thermos.

4. Each group then fills the thermos about ¾ of the way with the hottest tap water (105 to 110 degrees Fahrenheit), covering the jar. Each then screws on the thermos top.

5. Have students leave their thermoses in a safe spot for at least three to four hours. Students then open their thermoses and take out their jars, which they open and stir.

7. Then write the following questions on the board and ask students, with their groups, to answer and hand in the questions that follow. They should use class notes and the Internet to help with the classification levels.

    a. Observe the change in the milk mixture. What adjectives would you use to describe the new product?

    b. What do you think happened to the milk?

    c. How did the live yogurt cultures thicken the milk?

    d. How did the bacteria reproduce to form yogurt?

    e. How would yogurt be classified using the scientific classification system?

How to Adapt This Lab for the Inclusive Classroom

For Students with Visual Difficulties

Type the yogurt recipe ahead of time using a large, bold font to make students' reading easier while they are working.

For Students with Physical Disabilities

For the wheelchair-bound student, place a cutting board over the wheelchair to serve as a desk, on which he or she can stir the yogurt cultures and honey together before they are added to the saucepan. Other jobs, such as securing the thermos, also can be done here.

Home/School Connection

Give students the following assignment to complete at home:

I will assign you a plant, animal, protist, or fungus from the domain Eukarya. Research pertinent information on, and the levels of classification for, your organism for an oral presentation you will make to the class. Use note cards and at least one visual aid in this presentation.

How to Evaluate This Lesson

Use a project-based assessment of the Home/School Connection presentation. Base the grade on organization and accuracy of factual information, the student's knowledge of classification levels, and the quality of the visual aid.

Activity 2: The Structure and Function of Cells

Purpose: Students will learn about the functions and parts of the cell.

Read through the lesson and the adaptations and make sure you have the supplies you will need.

Supplies for the main lesson

chalkboard, overhead projector, computer with presentation software, or interactive whiteboard

science notebooks

Supplies for the adaptations

index cards

assorted colored markers

colored construction paper

large-font class notes and worksheets

blank cell diagrams

Lesson

1. Begin by saying something like, "Today we are going to learn about cells and their functions. Cells are the basic building blocks of all living things. The way cells replicate themselves and interact with one another determines how an organism is created and lives. Basic cell theory consists of three main premises: cells are the basic units that create form and function in all living things, all living things are made of cells, and all cells come from other cells."

2. On the board, show a diagram of the parts of a cell and explain that both plant and animal cells contain the defined parts. Write the following definitions for students to copy down in their notebooks:

   a. **Cell Membrane:** The cell membrane is the outer boundary of the cell. It serves as a protective barrier, allowing only certain materials to flow in and out of the cell.

   b. **Nucleus:** The nucleus is the heart of the cell. It houses the DNA and chromosomes.

   c. **Cytoplasm:** The cytoplasm is the material in the cell that contains the nutrients and water to keep the cell healthy.

   d. **Nuclear Membrane:** This thin structure separates the cell's nucleus from the cytoplasm.

   e. **Endoplasmic Reticulum:** The endoplasmic reticulum moves all nutrients and materials around the cell.

   f. **Ribosomes:** Ribosomes make protein for the cell.

   g. **Golgi Bodies:** Golgi bodies package the proteins in the cell and bring them to the outer parts of the cell.

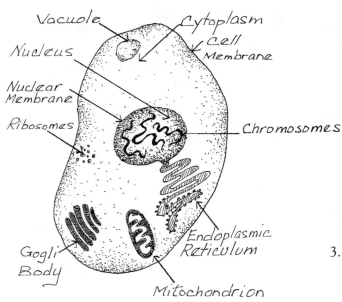

h. **Mitochondria:** Mitochondria break down food into energy for the cell.

i. **Vacuoles:** The vacuoles provide storage areas within the cell.

j. **DNA (deoxyribonucleic acid):** DNA is the hereditary material in humans and almost all other organisms. Most DNA is located in the cell nucleus, but a small amount of DNA can also be found in the mitochondria.

k. **Chromosomes:** Chromosomes are the organized structure of DNA and protein that is found in cells.

3. Inform students that plant cells also include the following parts, in addition to those above:

a. **Cell Wall:** The cell wall is a strong layer of nonliving material that protects the cell.

b. **Chloroplasts:** Chloroplasts contain chlorophyll, a green pigment, which makes food for the plant cells.

Hand out the Structure and Function of Cells Worksheet and proceed to work with small groups of students on some of the adaptations. Also, if time permits, have the students participate in the Whole Class Lab at the end of this activity.

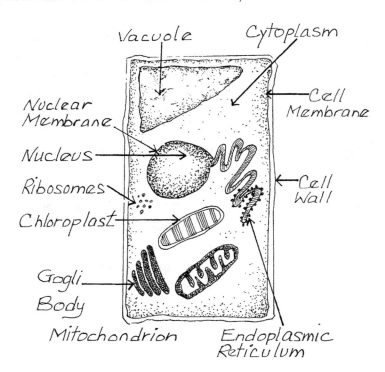

Structure and Function of Cells Worksheet

Match the definition in column B to the term in column A.

A	B
1. ____ Chloroplast	a. Houses DNA and chromosomes
2. ____ Ribosomes	b. Outer boundary of the cell
3. ____ Vacuoles	c. Separates the nucleus from cytoplasm
4. ____ Cell Wall	d. Makes food for plant cells
5. ____ Cytoplasm	e. Protects the cell
6. ____ Mitochondria	f. Provide the storage areas in the cell
7. ____ Cell Membrane	g. Make protein for the cell
8. ____ Nucleus	h. Break down food into energy
9. ____ Golgi Bodies	i. Material in cell that contains nutrients
10. ____ Endoplasmic Reticulum	j. Bring proteins to outer parts of the cell
11. ____ Nuclear Membrane	k. Moves all nutrients around the cell

12. Three components of basic cell theory are:

_____

_____

_____

How to Adapt This Lesson for the Inclusive Classroom
For Learning Disabled Students
Review each definition with a small group of students. To facilitate learning the parts of the cell, have students in the group take twelve index cards each. On one side of the index cards, have students write the names of cell parts with a brightly colored marker. On the other side, have students write down a few key words that will help them remember each cell part's structure or function. Students may also draw pictures on the back of the index cards that will aid as memory devices. Students can now form pairs and quiz each other on cell vocabulary and definitions. Once they have mastered these concepts, they can proceed to the worksheet. Students can also label blank diagrams of cells that you provide.

For Students with Visual or Perceptual Difficulties
Type class notes and worksheets in a large font and print them ahead of time for easier viewing. Also, students can use construction paper to block out extraneous text while reading definitions.

For Students with Cognitive Difficulties
Using the class notes, work with these students in small groups and use the note card strategy mentioned in the Learning Disabled Students activity above, having students learn only half of the definitions at one time. When students have mastered these definitions, proceed to the rest of the list.

For Gifted Learners
Everyone has seen the game "Who Wants to Be a Millionaire?" on television. Expand on this lesson by having gifted students design a game that resembles this TV game show called "Who Wants to be a Cellionaire?" Students will create questions at varying difficulty levels. As participants successfully answer a question, they move up in difficulty and corresponding reward potential. Students may include class and worksheet information from Activities 1 and 2 in this chapter, also using the Internet to design more difficult questions. This game can be played with the whole class as a review. It may also be modified such that groups of four or five students answer questions collectively. Include prizes at each level, such as a pencil, pen, bookmark, homework pass, or ice cream and pizza party, as students answer more difficult questions.

For Resistant Learners or Students with ADD/ADHD
To engage students with behavioral difficulties, allow them to lead several rounds of Who Wants to Be a Cellionaire? by having them quiz other contestants or keep score.

Whole Class Lab: Make a Cell Poster
Purpose: Students will create a visual representation of the parts and functions of the cell. This lab works best with groups of three to four students.

Supplies (per group)
copies of animal and plant cell diagrams from this book

two pieces of poster board

piece of colored foam board

curling ribbon

glitter

buttons

construction paper

yarn

colored markers

crayons

glue

scissors

1. Have students use the diagrams provided in this activity and the supplies listed above to make plant and animal cell posters, with different materials representing different parts of the cell.

2. Once they have completed the posters, students should write a paragraph that explains how the cell functions. Ask students to hand in the completed posters and essays for group lab grades.

How to Adapt This Lab for the Inclusive Classroom

For Learning Disabled Students

Instead of having students decide which materials may best represent cell parts, have two completed posters for students to replicate.

For Students with Visual Difficulties

Enlarge the cell pictures to aid these students in viewing cell parts while they work on their group posters.

For Students with Fine Motor or Perceptual Difficulties

Sometimes using scissors is difficult for students with these difficulties. Have students work in a group with more artistic students who can draw and cut, whereas those with difficulties can plan, paste, and color the parts of the cell.

For Students with Physical Disabilities

If a student is wheelchair bound, make sure the table is at a height where he or she can actively participate. If the tables are not at the right height, place a cutting board or piece of wood across the wheelchair to form a desk.

Home/School Connection

Give students the following assignment to complete at home:

Have your family help you write a poem about the structure and functions of cells. Bring in the completed poem to share with the class.

How to Evaluate This Lesson

Use a traditional evaluation for this lesson. For a quiz, give each student an unlabeled diagram of a plant and an animal cell, and have him or her label the parts in each diagram.

Activity 3: Cell Division—Mitosis

Purpose: Students will understand how cells divide and grow through the process of mitosis. Read through the lesson and the adaptations and make sure you have the supplies you will need.

Supplies for the main lesson

chalkboard, overhead projector, computer with presentation software, or interactive whiteboard

science notebooks

Supplies for the adaptations

poster board

flip chart

assorted colored markers

egg timer

copies of the worksheets

Lesson

1. Begin by saying something like, "Today we are going to learn about mitosis. Cells split and divide in mitosis to continue the growth and development of the organism. For example, the nuclei of skin cells will split through mitosis, creating new skin cells to replace ones that have died. Mitosis has nothing to do with sexual reproduction. This reproductive process is called meiosis, and will be discussed in the next lesson."

2. Explain the phases of mitosis, in which cells divide. Write the definitions of the following phases on the board and have students take notes in their notebooks:

   a. **Interphase:** In this first phase of mitosis, the cell grows and obtains nutrients to gain strength. Once fully grown, the cell begins to copy the DNA found in the nucleus. This is very important, because all future cells must have a complete set of DNA with all of the cell's information in order to survive. The interphase takes the longest to complete.

   b. **Prophase:** In this second stage of mitosis, the chromosomes (organized structures of DNA and protein that are found in cells) in the nucleus condense and move to opposite sides of the nucleus. Thin spindles (organized arrays of microtubules that interact with the chromosomes) form around the chromosomes and make a bridge between both sides of the cell.

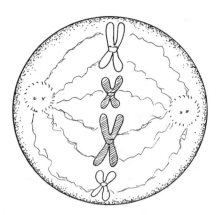

c. **Metaphase:** In this third stage, the chromosomes line up in the middle of the cell, preparing to separate.

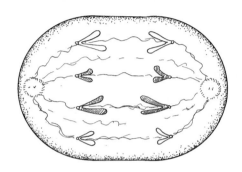

d. **Anaphase:** In anaphase, the aligned chromosomes are each pulled to opposite ends of the cell. Chromosomes equally divide themselves, resulting in identical features at each end of the cell. Lastly, the cell stretches out to form a rodlike shape.

e. **Telephase:** In this last phase of cell division, the chromosomes stretch out and lose their rod-like appearance. A new nucleus is formed at each end of the cell that encases the divided chromosomes. The cell, which now resembles a peanut, splits in the middle, forming two new, identical daughter cells. The cycle is now complete, and begins again.

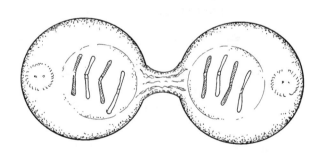

3. Discuss these phases and make sure students are clear about them before proceeding.

Hand out the Cell Division Worksheet and proceed to work with small groups of students on some of the adaptations. Also, if time permits, have the students participate in the Whole Class Lab at the end of this activity.

Cell Division Worksheet

Using complete sentences, and in your own words, complete the following questions.

1. Explain the process of mitosis.

   _____

   _____

   _____

2. Explain the first phase of cell division and why cells stay in this phase the longest.

   _____

   _____

   _____

3. What begins to happen in prophase?

   _____

   _____

   _____

4. Explain the third phase of cell division in mitosis.

   _____

   _____

   _____

5. The last phase of cell division in mitosis is telephase. Explain in detail what happens as a result of the completion of the cell division cycle.

   _____

   _____

   _____

How to Adapt This Lesson for the Inclusive Classroom

For Learning Disabled Students

Hand out additional copies of the worksheet without lines so that students may draw pictures to show their understanding. Review the process of mitosis with students and reteach the concepts pertaining to cell division. After the review, students can play It's Only a Phase, a memory game for four to six players.

It's Only a Phase

1. To set up the game, draw a picture of each phase of mitosis on a flip chart. Make sure pictures resemble class notes. Draw each diagram in a different color. Do not label the phases.

2. To begin the game, turn to one of the pictures, turn over the egg timer, and ask a student to name and explain the stage of mitosis in detail. If the student gives the correct answer before the egg timer runs out, he or she receives five points. If the answer is partially correct, the student receives three points. The next player then has a turn. Keep playing the game until it is evident that students understand the information.

3. The student with the most points is the winner.

For students who continue to struggle with the concept, use poster board to make a graphic organizer that provides a visual explanation of mitosis.

For Resistant Learners or Students with ADD/ADHD

To keep students with behavioral difficulties engaged in learning about mitosis, encourage them to participate in the above game, because it is fast paced, interactive, and fun.

For Gifted Learners

Expand on this lesson by having gifted students work in a small group to research mitosis as it applies to cancer research, aging, or cell mutations. Allow these students to take a trip to the computer lab and use the Internet to research these topics. They can then present this information to the class.

Whole Class Lab: The Bread of Life

Purpose: Students will learn about mitosis and cell reproduction by observing the growth of yeast.

This lab works best with groups of four students.

Supplies (per group)

two graduated 2-cup measuring cups

two packages of active dry yeast

set of measuring spoons

white lined paper

water

sugar

1. Have each group of students fill one measuring cup with 1 cup of cold water. They then sprinkle one yeast packet over the top of each cup.

2. Ask groups to fill their second measuring cups with very warm water. Each group then adds one tablespoon of sugar to the warm water, stirring to dissolve. They then sprinkle their second packet of yeast on top of the water.

3. Students then allow their cups to sit for five minutes.

4. Each group of students should observe the contents in their cups, explain what has happened in each cup, and hypothesize about how certain conditions in one cup allowed cell reproduction to occur. Students should brainstorm their theories and write group essays to hand in for their lab grades.

How to Adapt This Lab for the Inclusive Classroom
For Students with Fine Motor or Perceptual Difficulties

Tasks that require precision, such as measuring, should be avoided. Such tasks as sprinkling the yeast and making a hypothesis, however, are wonderful for these students.

Home/School Connection

Give students the following assignment to complete at home:

> With your family's help, develop a comic strip that explains the process of mitosis. Bring the finished comic into class to hang in the classroom and share with other students.

How to Evaluate This Lesson

For this lesson, we suggest using traditional assessment methods, evaluating the graded worksheet, the completed Home/School Connection project, and the quality of the group lab essay.

Activity 4: Cell Division—Meiosis

Purpose: Students will understand how cells divide through the process of meiosis. Read through the lesson and the adaptations and make sure you have the supplies you will need.

Supplies for the main lesson

chalkboard, overhead projector, computer with presentation software, or interactive whiteboard

science notebooks

Supplies for the adaptations

Internet access

Lesson

1. Begin by saying something like, "Today we are going to learn about meiosis. Meiosis is the process of cell division in which chromosome pairs split and form a new egg and sperm, or sex cells. These sex cells have only half the amount of chromosomes of the parent cell. Reproduction of the species occurs at conception, when the sperm and egg cells unite.

2. Explain the phases of meiosis and display illustrations using your computer and LCD or overhead. Write the two phases below on the board and have students take notes in their notebooks:

   a. **Phase I:** In the first stage of meiosis, the cell replicates its chromosomes. DNA, or genes, are found on chromosomes. Every chromosome is copied from the parent cell, doubling the amount of information inside the cell. Chromosomes attach to spindles, cross over, and pair up at the center of the cell. The cell splits in two, each new cell having half of the new chromosome pairs.

   b. **Phase II:** In each split cell, the chromosomes again move to the center of the cell. Chromosomes attach to spindles, again crossing over to form new pairs. Each pair then goes to opposite ends of the cells. Cells divide in half again, producing four sex cells. Each cell has half the number of chromosomes of each of the parent cells.

One of 23 homologous pairs

Replication (Interphase)

Metaphase I

Metaphase II   Metaphase II

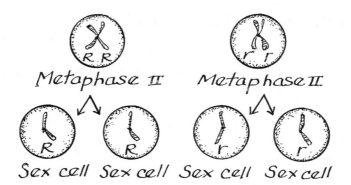

Metaphase II   Metaphase II

Sex cell Sex cell Sex cell Sex cell

3. Discuss these phases and make sure students are clear about them before proceeding.

Hand out the Meiosis Worksheet and proceed to work with small groups of students on some of the adaptations. Also, if time permits, have the students participate in the Whole Class Lab at the end of this activity.

Name: _____   Date: _____

Meiosis Worksheet

Circle the best answer for the following multiple choice questions.

1. Chromosomes are composed of:
   a. genes
   b. parent cells
   c. sperm
   d. DNA

2. In meiosis, cells split, forming sex cells with:
   a. twice as many chromosomes
   b. strands of DNA
   c. half the amount of chromosomes
   d. spindles

3. In meiosis, the parent cell splits:
   a. three times
   b. two times
   c. four times
   d. one time

4. The process of meiosis best explains the process of:
   a. osmosis
   b. reproduction
   c. mutations
   d. mitosis

5. In your own words, and using complete sentences, explain the process of meiosis.

   _____

   _____

   _____

   _____

   _____

   _____

How to Adapt This Lesson for the Inclusive Classroom
For Learning Disabled Students
Review the notes taken in class and the vocabulary terms below using the FIRST Strategy:

meiosis	chromosome	DNA	sperm	genes
egg	parent cell	species	spindles	sex cell

The FIRST Strategy

F = First. Review and reteach the vocabulary words listed.

I = Internet. Supervise students as they further research the vocabulary words on the Internet.

R = Review. Have students review their Internet findings with the group.

S = Students. Have students state their own definitions of the words. Groups can agree on the most suitable definitions.

T = Teacher. Write the definitions on the board so students can refer to them while working on the worksheet.

You may also suggest that the students cover up the multiple choice answers with a piece of paper or their hands, first answering the question themselves before looking for the answer from among the choices.

For Students with Fine Motor or Perceptual Difficulties
Students may answer question 5 in bullet points to minimize handwriting. Students may also use the keyboard to answer question 5 and attach their answers to the worksheet.

For Students with Visual Difficulties
Students may use a piece of paper to cover any text on the page, other than the question on which they are working; to minimize the visual processing required.

For Gifted Learners
Expand on this lesson by having gifted students develop a PowerPoint presentation or dramatization of meiosis and sex cell reproduction to share with the class.

Whole Class Lab: Edible Cell Division
Purpose: Students will further understand and visualize the process of meiosis.
Students should work individually for this experiment.

Supplies (per student)
five Nilla Wafers

small cup of prepared vanilla icing

handful of mini–chocolate chips

tube of writer's icing

plastic knife

piece of waxed paper

diagram of edible cell

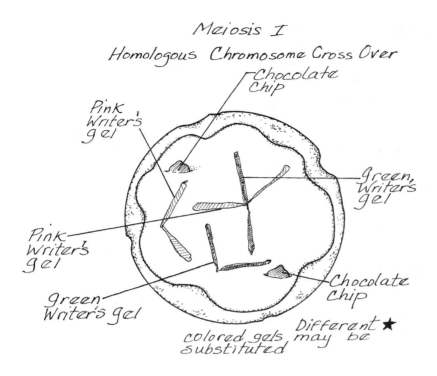

Meiosis I
Homologous Chromosome Cross Over

Chocolate Chip

Pink Writer's gel

Green Writer's gel

Pink Writer's gel

Green Writer's gel

Chocolate Chip

colored gels may be Different ★ substituted

1. Have students wash their hands.

2. Instruct students that they will be using the pictures provided in the class notes to make edible diagrams of each stage of meiosis.

3. Students should ice each cookie using their plastic knives.

4. They then break the cookies in halves or fourths to depict certain stages.

5. Students can draw spindles with writer's icing, using the mini chocolate chips as the chromosomes.

6. They should lay out the edible diagrams on waxed paper and label each part of the process. When finished, place the cookies on display for all to see. Then the class can eat and enjoy!

How to Adapt This Lab for the Inclusive Classroom

For Learning Disabled Students

Work on the edible cells in small groups to model the process step by step, or provide the students with a diagram.

For Students with Fine Motor or Perceptual Difficulties

These students each can work with a more dexterous student as a team effort to complete their cell projects.

Home/School Connection

Give students the following assignment to complete at home:

With your family's help, find copies of pictures that show the different phases of meiosis, and use those pictures to create a poster depicting the complete process. Bring your poster in to display in the classroom.

How to Evaluate This Lesson

If possible, use an interview format. Talk to each student individually, asking him or her to explain the process of meiosis in his or her own words.

Activity 5: Heredity and Genetics

Purpose: Students will develop a broad understanding of genes and their impact on inherited traits.

Read through the lesson and the adaptations and make sure you have the supplies you will need.

Supplies for the main lesson

chalkboard, overhead projector, computer with presentation software, or interactive whiteboard

index cards

science notebooks

Supplies for the adaptations

construction paper

red and blue Lego bricks

unlined white paper

index cards

Lesson

1. Pass out an index card to each student before the lesson begins. Ask students to write the eye colors of both of their parents on one side of the cards, and their own eye colors on the other.

2. Next say something like, "Today we are going to learn about heredity and genetics. When speaking about heredity, you are speaking about traits that have been passed down from parents through genes. Genes can be dominant, such as that leading to brown eyes, or recessive, such as those resulting in blue eyes or baldness. The study of genes is called genetics."

3. Then say, "Some traits are controlled by one dominant and one recessive gene. When these genes pair, they are called alleles. Eye color and sex, for example, are characteristics each determined by a single gene.

   "Other characteristics are controlled by single genes with more than two outcomes, or multiple alleles. In regard to hair color, for example, hair can be blonde, shades of brown, black, or white. Another example involves blood type. Blood types can be classified as A+, A–, B+, B– AB+, AB–,O+, or O–.

   "Lastly, other genes work together with many genes to form a single trait, such as height. That is why you can be similar in height to your grandmother, grandfather, aunt, uncle, mother, or father."

4. Explain Punnett squares, saying, "A Punnett square is a square diagram that can indicate all the possibilities of a genetic cross. It shows the probability of an inherited trait. For example, if your mom has blue eyes (bb) and your dad has brown with a recessive blue gene (Bb), a Punnett square would be filled in like this," and draw the following on the board:

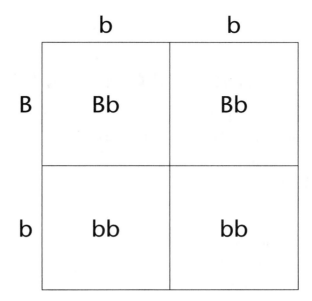

Then explain, "In this Punnett square, you would have a 50 percent chance of having bb (blue eyes) and a 50 percent chance of having Bb (brown eyes)."

5. Have students take out their notebooks. Ask each to use the information on his or her index card to draw a Punnett square based on the previous example.

6. Ask several students to come to the board to draw their Punnett squares. Students should explain their findings and generate a class discussion.

Hand out the Heredity and Genetics Worksheet and proceed to work with small groups of students on some of the adaptations. Also, if time permits, have the students participate in the Whole Class Lab at the end of this activity.

Heredity and Genetics Worksheet

Circle the best answer to complete each item.

1. The study of dominant and recessive genes is called:
   a. inheritance
   b. inherited characteristics
   c. heredity
   d. genetics

2. A Punnett square shows:
   a. the probability of an inherited trait
   b. eye color characteristics
   c. gene pairs
   d. traits passed down through generations

3. An example of a trait resulting from multiple alleles is:
   a. height
   b. blood type
   c. weight
   d. widow's peak

4. Alleles are:
   a. recessive genes
   b. dominant genes
   c. gene pairs
   d. chromosomes

5 Fill in each Punnett square. Underneath each square, write down the probability out of four possible outcomes that each trait is likely to occur.

a. Eye color—BB (brown eyes) and bb (blue eyes)

b. Gender—XX (male) and XY (female)

How to Adapt This Lesson for the Inclusive Classroom

For Learning Disabled Students

Review new or unfamiliar vocabulary and generate a small-group discussion to ensure understanding of words.

Multiple choice questions can be answered using self-talk. Students may cover items not being worked on with a bookmark or piece of construction paper to minimize distractions. For the Punnett squares, students can work with a white sheet of paper, folded into four sections, and red and blue Lego bricks. For example, a blue brick can represent b and a red brick could represent B. Model how to fill in the squares with the bricks. When students understand the crossing-over concept with blocks, have them move on to examining eye color and gender genes.

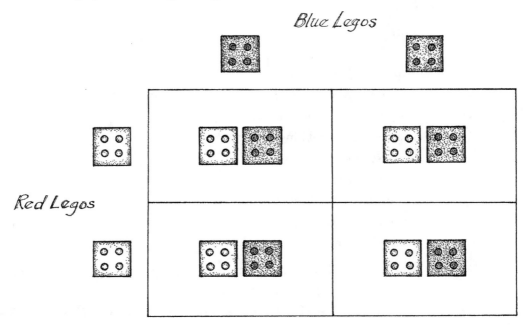

For Delayed Readers

Break down unknown words phonetically for the students. Allow them to tap syllables on the desk with a pencil, then pronounce the words. Once they have pronounced the words correctly, have students read each item on the worksheet aloud before answering the questions.

For Resistant Learners or Students with ADD/ADHD

Pair these students with classmates who understand the concept of Punnett squares. Draw blank Punnett squares on index cards. Hand these out along with examples of Punnett squares for eye color. Get students engaged in this activity by having each pair take turns filling out the squares and determining the probability that the inherited trait will occur.

For Gifted Learners

Expand on this lesson by having gifted learners use the Internet to research genetic engineering or cloning. Students can prepare questions and organize a debate to present in the classroom.

Whole Class Lab: Observing DNA

Purpose: Students will observe DNA by extracting DNA from strawberries. This lab works best with groups of four to six students.

Supplies (teacher)

four strawberries (washed, dried, and with tops cut off)

¼ teaspoon of salt

1 cup of water

blender

strainer

knife

whisk

Supplies (per group)

2 tablespoons of liquid dishwashing detergent

½ teaspoon of meat tenderizer

1 tablespoon of rubbing alcohol

two test tubes

measuring spoons

measuring cup or beaker to pour ingredients

two coffee stirrers

unlined paper

1. Cut the strawberries into slices. Then add strawberries, salt, and water to the blenders and puree the strawberries.

2. Next pour strawberries into strainers over bowls to strain out the seeds. Divide the strawberry mixture among the groups, with two test tubes per group.

3. Have students add dishwashing detergent to their strawberries and whisk. The mixtures should sit undisturbed for fifteen minutes, during which time the soap traps the cells of the strawberries by forming bubbles.

4. Students should fill test tubes with the mixture until they are ⅓ full.

5. Students add ⅛ of a teaspoon of meat tenderizer (an enzyme) to each of the test tubes, lightly stirring with coffee stirrers. The enzymes separate the proteins from the DNA, making the DNA much easier to see with the naked eye.

6. Groups should fill another ⅓ of their test tubes with rubbing alcohol. The tube is now ⅔ full of solution. It should lie on the top of each tube. Have students look for a stringy substance between the alcohol and strawberry juice. DNA molecules make up this substance. Students should observe that these molecules are very long and stringy.

7. Using unlined paper, each group should draw, label, and hand in a picture of their results concerning the strawberry DNA.

How to Adapt This Lab for the Inclusive Classroom

For Students with Fine Motor or Perceptual Difficulties

Allow these students to participate in steps that don't require fine motor skills, such as cutting strawberries or pouring liquids into the test tubes.

For Resistant Learners or Students with ADD/ADHD

Circle the room, making sure these students are engaged in interactive tasks during the lab. Difficulties sometimes occur in small-group labs when students do not have enough jobs to complete.

Home/School Connection

Give students the following assignment to complete at home:

> Find an article online or in the newspaper regarding genetic disorders. Discuss your findings with your family and write a one-page reaction. Hand in the report and a copy of the article.

How to Evaluate This Lesson

For this lesson, we suggest you have students work with their lab group to create a poster for you to assess their learning. It may include vocabulary, diagrams of Punnett squares, and whatever else their creativity inspires. If needed, you can assign group roles or have each student use a different color on the poster to ensure that all participate. Have the students present their completed posters to the rest of the class.

Activity 6: Plants

Purpose: Students will learn about the structure and functions of plant systems.

Read through the lesson and the adaptations and make sure you have the supplies you will need.

Supplies for the main lesson

chalkboard, overhead projector, computer with presentation software, or interactive whiteboard

science notebooks

Supplies for the adaptations

index cards

assorted colored markers

assorted colored highlighters

construction paper

copies of class notes

extra copies of the worksheet

Lesson

1. Begin by saying something like, "Today we are going to learn about plants. There are two major groups of plants. They are called nonvascular and vascular plants. Can anyone tell me anything about either of these types?" Facilitate a class discussion.

2. Write the following definitions on the board and have students take notes in their notebooks:

   a. **Nonvascular Plants:** Nonvascular plants are plants that grow on the ground as a ground cover. They do not have roots that feed the rest of the plant structure by absorbing water from the ground. Instead, these plants obtain their nutrients and water from the air, the ground, and each other, and pass these nutrients from cell to cell. Examples of nonvascular plants are mosses, hornworts, and liverworts. They typically live in dark, moist, or shady places.

   b. **Vascular Plants:** Vascular plants have tubes made of cells in the roots, stems, and leaves that nourish them with food and water to live and grow. Examples of vascular plants are flowering plants and trees.

2. Begin the next part of the lesson by asking students if anyone has ever grown a garden at home. Ask the students with what plants they have had the most success.

   Now say, "Most of the plants we have discussed that have grown in your gardens are called seed plants. They are among the most common plants on the planet."

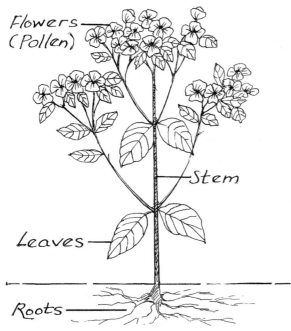

Parts of a Seed Plant

Flowers (Pollen)

Stem

Leaves

Roots

3. Write the following characteristics of seed plants on the board for students to copy down in their notebooks:

   a. They have a vascular system, meaning they have roots, stems, and leaves with tubes that transport food and oxygen throughout each plant.

   b. They need pollen to reproduce. Pollen is usually transported by insects, and by bees in particular. Once seeds reproduce, they are transported by the elements, animals, birds, or water.

4. Explain the process of photosynthesis, saying, "Photosynthesis is the process by which green plants use solar energy to convert water, carbon dioxide, and minerals into chemical compounds necessary for survival. In simpler terms, this energy is used to make food for the plants.

"It happens this way: when it rains, the roots of green plants absorb water from the ground. Water is stored in the roots, and then travels through the tubes to the stems and leaves. When water reaches the leaves, it mixes with carbon dioxide. The leaves get carbon dioxide from the air. Water and carbon dioxide go to the plant cells, which contain chlorophyll. When the light from the sun hits this mixture, the chlorophyll helps convert it into a form of sugar, which is stored in the leaves. The plants then use this food as needed. The plants release oxygen as a byproduct from this reaction.

"We are codependent with plants for survival: plants both provide us with food and release oxygen, which is essential for human life, and we in turn release carbon dioxide, on which the plant kingdom relies."

Hand out the Plants Worksheet and proceed to work with small groups of students on some of the adaptations. Also, if time permits, have the students participate in the Whole Class Lab at the end of this activity.

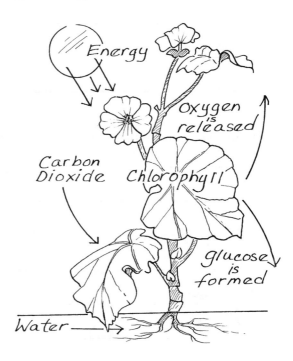

Energy

Oxygen is released

Carbon Dioxide

Chlorophyll

glucose is formed

Water

Name: _____ Date: _____

Plants Worksheet

Write short answers in the spaces provided below.

1. Briefly describe the differences between a vascular and a nonvascular plant.

   _____

   _____

   _____

2. Three examples of nonvascular plants are:

   _____, _____, and _____.

3. Three examples of seed plants are:

   _____, _____, and _____.

4. Two characteristics of seed plants are:

   _____

   _____

   _____

5. In your own words, explain the cycle of photosynthesis.

   _____

   _____

   _____

   _____

   _____

   _____

168

How to Adapt This Lesson for the Inclusive Classroom

For Learning Disabled Students

Review and reteach the notes with the students. Try the Read-Aloud Strategy for reinforcing concepts.

The Read-Aloud Strategy

1. Pass a copy of the class notes to each student, along with copies of the worksheet. Read the first worksheet question aloud to the group, and point to a general area of the notes where the answer may be found.

2. Have a student read that section of notes aloud, and discuss the material with the group.

3. Then ask the group to answer the worksheet question. When the group agrees on the answer, have each student highlight the particular section of notes where the answer may be found.

4. Continue, with students answering the remaining questions. This activity will provide a reference for students when they are completing their worksheets independently.

It should be noted that sometimes concepts are hard to grasp because they have multiple steps and are abstract. Try the following strategy for question 5, concerning photosynthesis. Students can break this concept into simple ideas by using index cards. With these students, review the definition of photosynthesis presented in class and the items written below. Then have students write each of these items on separate index cards.

Photosynthesis—How Do Plants Make Their Own Food?

1. Green plants need sun, water, and air to make food.

2. The sun's energy is absorbed by chlorophyll in the plant.

3. The chlorophyll converts water and carbon dioxide from the air into a form of sugar.

    Sun + water (through the roots) + carbon dioxide (from the air) = sugar.

4. The sugar is stored in the leaves and feeds the plants.

5. The plants give off oxygen as a byproduct.

On each index card, students may also draw a picture with colored markers that will aid them in remembering the sequence. If they are not sure what to draw, give them ideas for each item. Allow students to work in pairs, reviewing and quizzing one another. Once students have mastered the sequence, aid them in linking these sentences together to form single paragraphs. Students can use their paragraphs as answers on their worksheets.

For Students with Fine Motor or Perceptual Difficulties

Students may take notes using a graphic organizer or partial notes outline. Allow these students to type their answers using a keyboard and attach them to their worksheets. If this is not possible, you or a paraprofessional may scribe students' answers.

For Delayed Readers

Give each student a copy of the class notes, a bookmark, and a colored highlighter. Read each worksheet item. Have students take turns reading the corresponding section of the notes aloud, using the bookmark to follow along. Correct any mistakes students make on the worksheet, and have them mark their corrections with their highlighters. Ask students to reread the section of notes again and discuss their answers to the worksheet.

For Resistant Learners or Students with ADD/ADHD

If students with ADD/ADHD are struggling to focus and sustain attention, it may be because there is so much information to remember in this lesson. Allow students to work and review concepts with learning disabled students, with whom the strategies being used are fast paced, interactive, and fun.

For Gifted Learners

Expand on this lesson by having gifted students make a skit or movie titled "Let's Go Green," focusing on our planet's interdependence between plants and the condition of the environment. This skit can be serious or comical, and may include other members of the class. Students can also use props and background music. Students may record their skit or present it live to the class.

Whole Class Lab: See the Light

Purpose: Students will observe how light and water have an impact on plant growth and survival.

This lab is best performed in groups of four to six students.

Supplies (per group)

three half-dozen egg containers

four to five cups of potting soil

package of sunflower or green bean seeds

masking tape

permanent marker

tablespoon

piece of graphing paper

1. Have students fill each of their three egg cartons ¾ full with potting soil.

2. Each group should spoon out 1 tablespoon of soil from each division in the carton. They should then place one seed in each hole and cover this with soil.

3. Students should use masking tape to label the cartons as follows:

   Carton 1—Full sun and water

   Carton 2—Sun and water every other day

   Carton 3—No sun or water

4. Have each group place carton 1 near a sunny window and carton 3 in a dark spot where no sunlight can reach it.

1. Full Sun and Water

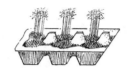

2. Sun and Water Every Other Day

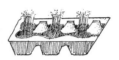

3. No Sun or Water

5. At the outset, students should water cartons 1 and 2. Over a period of two weeks, each group waters carton 1 every day and carton 2 every other day. Students do not water carton 3.

6. Have each group place carton 2 with carton 1 on even-numbered days, and with carton 3 on odd-numbered days.

7. Students should chart the results for the two weeks on graphing paper.

8. At the end of two weeks, ask students to write a summary of the results with their groups to share with the class. They should address whether plants thrive and grow with a lot of sun and water, minimal sun and water, or no sun and water.

How to Adapt This Lab for the Inclusive Classroom

For Resistant Learners or Students with ADD/ADHD

Allow these students to be responsible for checking the plants and watering them during the two-week time frame. This task requires responsibility and will serve to build self-esteem, while allowing students to get up and walk around the classroom.

For Students with Physical Disabilities

Allow these students also to care for the plants during the two-week time frame. These students are often excluded from jobs requiring responsibility because of physical limitations. Pair these students with resistant learners, allowing them to water and rotate the seedling cartons together

Home/School Connection

Have students complete the following assignment at home:

Research and design a poster that describes one or more things that can be done at home to aid in protecting the plants on our planet. Try to convince viewers that they should do these things. Bring the completed poster into class.

How to Evaluate This Lesson

We recommend using an individual interview, the completed worksheet, lab participation, and the Home/School Connection poster as parts of each student's final grade, as follows:

Interview	25 percent
Worksheet	25 percent
Lab participation	25 percent
Home/School Connection poster	25 percent

Chapter 8

The Human Body

Activity 1: The Skeletal System, Joints, and Muscles

Purpose: Students will learn how bones, joints, and muscles work together.

Read through the lesson and the adaptations and make sure you have the supplies you will need.

Supplies for the main lesson

chalkboard, overhead projector, computer with presentation software, or interactive whiteboard

science notebooks

picture, poster, or model of the human skeletal system

Internet access

For the adaptations

poster board

red, green, and amber colored paper

glue stick

scissors

Internet access

Lesson

1. Begin by saying something like, "Today we are going to talk about your bones, joints, and muscles, also known as the musculoskeletal system. First we will focus on your bones. These are part of what is called the skeletal system."

2. Use the picture of the skeletal system throughout the lesson to point out the different features. Have students take notes in their notebooks.

   Explain that the human skeletal system is made up of bones, cartilage, tendons, and ligaments and has the following six major functions:

   a. It protects the internal organs. An example of this is the skull, which protects the brain.

   b. It makes red blood cells. These are made in the bone marrow found in the center of larger bones, such as the pelvis.

   c. It stores minerals for the body's future use. The most common minerals stored in the bones are calcium and magnesium.

   d. It helps your body move.

   e. It provides a structure to which muscles, ligaments, and tendons can attach.

   f. It provides shape and support to the body.

3. Next, talk about the joints. Joints are points in the body at which two or more bones connect. Joints come in two categories: nonmoveable and moveable.

   a. **Nonmoveable joints:** Nonmoveable joints are also called sutures. For example, the joints holding the bones of the skull together are immovable sutures.

b. **Moveable Joints:** Moveable joints allow two bones to move together without damaging each other. Examples of moveable joints are the knee, shoulder, and hip. Moveable joints are classified into four types:

> **Ball-and-Socket Joint:** This joint allows for the greatest amount of motion, letting the joint rotate, twist, and turn. Ball-and-socket joints are found in the shoulder and hip.

> **Hinge Joint:** A hinge joint moves back and forth, much as does a car door. Examples of hinge joints include the elbow, ankle, and knee.

> **Gliding Joint:** A gliding joint allows three different kinds of motion: linear motion, such as smooth sliding of bone past bone; angular motion, such as bending and stretching; and circular motion. An example of a gliding joint is found in the wrist.

> **Condyloid Joint:** A condyloid joint is where adjacent bones are joined by ligaments and other fibrous tissues. Examples of condyloid joint movement are seen in the bending of fingers and the nodding of the head.

4. Now explain the muscles, noting that they are categorized as either voluntary or involuntary. Note that there are three types of muscles in the body: skeletal muscles, cardiac muscles, and smooth muscles:

a. **Skeletal Muscles:** These are attached to your bones and provide strength. They are voluntary muscles because their movement can be controlled.

b. **Cardiac Muscles:** The cardiac muscle is found in the walls of the heart. It is considered involuntary because its movement is continuous and automatic. Coordinated contraction of cardiac muscle cells pumps blood through your body.

c. **Smooth Muscles:** Smooth muscles are involuntary muscles found inside of organs. They move automatically, allowing the systems of the body to function properly. Smooth muscles are found in the large and small intestines. The movements included in the process of digestion are considered involuntary movements.

5. If you have an Internet connection, go to www.visiblebody.com. Allow students to take the virtual tour of the skeletal system, joints, and muscles.

Hand out the Skeletal System, Joints, and Muscles Worksheet and proceed to work with small groups of students on some of the adaptations. Also, if time permits, have the students participate in the Whole Class Lab at the end of this activity.

Name: _____   Date: _____

Skeletal System, Joints, and Muscles Worksheet

Write the word True or False before each statement below.

1. _____ The skeletal system stores calcium and magnesium.

2. _____ An example of a ball-and-socket joint is the knee.

3. _____ Bone marrow makes red blood cells.

4. _____ The heart is a voluntary muscle.

5. _____ An example of a hinge joint is the ankle.

6. _____ Skeletal muscles are attached to your bones.

7. _____ The condyloid joint allows the head to nod.

8. _____ Movements in the digestive tract are considered voluntary movements.

9. _____ Providing shape and support is one function of the skeletal system.

10. _____ The hip is an example of a ball-and-socket joint.

How to Adapt This Lesson for the Inclusive Classroom

For Learning Disabled Students

Students can take notes using a graphic organizer or partial notes outline. Review the notes and terms aloud with a small group of students. Once the review is completed, students can use the Green Light Strategy to answer the true-or-false questions on the worksheet.

Green Light Strategy

1. Using a piece of poster board, make a picture of a traffic light, gluing red, amber, and green construction paper circles as the lights. Write the following words in each circle:

   Red   = Read.

   Amber = Ask yourself.

   Green = Go back and find.

2. For each item on the worksheet, students can use this strategy to determine the answer.

3. The red light tells students to read the true-or-false question aloud. The amber light instructs each student to ask himself or herself, "What do I think the answer is? Why? Is the question a trick question? What did I learn in class that makes me believe that the answer is true or false?" Students write their predicted answers on separate pieces of paper. Finally, the green light reminds students to go back to their notes, comparing what they find with their predicted answers. If their answers are correct, the light is green to go ahead and put these answers on their answer sheets.

For Students with Cognitive Difficulties

Reread and review the notes with students. Generate a discussion. Find simple pictures of joints, bones, and muscles to aid in understanding.

For Resistant Learners or Students with ADD/ADHD

Have each student pair up with a more advanced student and use the Green Light Strategy to review the material and answer the questions on the worksheet.

For Gifted Learners

Expand on this lesson by having gifted learners research various X-rays of human and animal skeletal systems on the Internet and prepare a slide show to share with the class. The other students can then guess what type of skeleton and what section of the body are being shown.

Whole Class Lab: Voluntary and Involuntary Muscles

Purpose: This lab will show students how voluntary and involuntary muscles work together. This lab works best with students in pairs.

Supplies (per pair)

digital watch, analog watch with a second hand, or stopwatch

paper and pencils

1. One student in each pair should take his or her own pulse. Explain to students, "A pulse is the rate your heart beats. A resting heart rate is the number of times your heart beats in one minute while at rest. To take your pulse, make sure you are sitting quietly for ten minutes. Then, place two fingers on your neck, close to your jaw. You will feel pulsing in the blood vessels here, because they are close to the skin's surface. Have your teammate time you for thirty seconds while you count the pulsing beats. Multiply the number by two. This is your resting heart rate.

2. Have the other partner use the same procedure to take his or her pulse.

3. Both partners should then stand up and reach over their heads.

4. Next, each partner should hop on one foot and then the other.

5. Finally, both partners should run in place.

6. Now have students try to change their heart rates. Ask them, "Can you make your heart rate change whenever you want to? Does your heart beat whether you think about it or not? How is your heart different from some of the other muscles in your body that you just used to raise your arms, hop on one foot, and run in place?"

7. Have students now take a working heart rate. One student in each pair first jogs or jumps in place for three minutes. The pair then retakes that student's pulse. Students should calculate their working heart rates, noticing the difference in the numbers between the resting and working pulse rates. The process should be repeated with the second partner taking his or her pulse.

8. After sitting quietly for a few minutes, students should take their pulses again. Each student should observe how his or her pulse has changed, and deduce why.

9. Students should write their reactions to this lab, expressing their conclusions about voluntary and involuntary muscles.

10. As a possible extension, pupils and the muscles that close the eyelids can further explain the interdependence of voluntary and involuntary muscles. If light is bright, the involuntary muscles of the pupil will contract, whereas the voluntary muscles of the eyelids cause them to close.

How to Adapt This Lab for the Inclusive Classroom

For Students with Physical Disabilities

If students are wheelchair bound, allow them to just move their arms up and down for three minutes before taking a working heart rate. For students with coordination concerns, simplify the exercise, or tailor the physical tasks to some they can comfortably execute.

Home/School Connection

Give the students the following assignment to complete at home:

With your family, look around your house and find examples of things that are similar to the different types of joints studied in class. For example, a door hinge would be a great visual example of a hinged joint. Write a one-page essay comparing how these items function to how the corresponding joints work in the human body. Bring the finished essay into class.

How to Evaluate This Lesson

We recommend a traditional assessment for this activity. Quiz the students on the information learned in class by rephrasing and changing the position of the worksheet items. Also, use the grades for the lab assignment and Home/School Connection essay as part of the total grade.

Activity 2: The Cardiovascular System

Purpose: Students will understand the purpose of the cardiovascular system and how it works.

Read through the lesson and the adaptations and make sure you have the supplies you will need.

Supplies for the main lesson

chalkboard, overhead projector, computer with presentation software, or interactive whiteboard

science notebooks

Supplies for the adaptations

note cards

assorted colored markers

flip chart

blank diagram of the heart

Lesson

1. Begin by saying something like, "Today we are going to learn about the cardiovascular system and the heart. This system is also called the circulatory system." Generate a discussion, asking the students to explain how they think the cardiovascular system functions in the body.

2. After the discussion, write the following definition on the board and have students take it down in their notebooks:

   The Cardiovascular System: This circulatory system is made up of the heart, blood vessels, and blood. Its main job is to carry nutrition and water to all cells and to carry waste products away. It also carries disease-preventing materials in the blood that circulate and strengthen the internal organs.

3. Then discuss the functions of the cardiovascular system in depth:

   a. It carries oxygen to the cells. When you inhale, oxygen enters your lungs. Your bloodstream picks up the oxygen and transmits it to the cells.

   b. It carries nutrients and glucose to the cells and internal organs. The digestive system breaks food down into glucose and nutrients, which enter the bloodstream and travel to all of the cells in the body.

   c. It spreads disease-fighting cells. Part of the blood carries specific cells that strengthen the immune system and attack disease-causing organisms.

   d. It removes waste from the cells. The blood picks up waste products from the cells. The waste is removed when you exhale, and exits the body as carbon dioxide.

4. Now talk about the heart, telling students that the heart is the main organ of the cardiovascular system. Write the following facts about the heart on the board and have students take notes in their notebooks:

a. The heart is approximately the size of your fist.

b. Blood cannot travel through the cardiovascular system without passing through the heart.

c. The heart is divided into a right and left side by a wall called the septum. Each side is divided into two chambers called the atria (left and right atrium) and the ventricles (left and right ventricle). The atria (upper chambers) receive blood that enters the heart. The ventricles (lower chambers) pump blood away from the heart.

d. Blood vessels that carry blood away from the heart are called arteries.

e. Blood vessels that carry blood back to the heart are called veins.

5. Now describe how the heart works, saying something like, "The right side of the heart collects blood with minimal oxygen availability (oxygen poor) from the body and pumps it to the lungs. The left side of the heart collects oxygen-rich blood from the lungs and pushes it out to the rest of the body. The heart beats in two stages: first the atria contract or draws together to pump blood from the atria to the ventricles. Then the ventricles contract to pump the blood throughout the body. The heart then relaxes and lets in more blood."

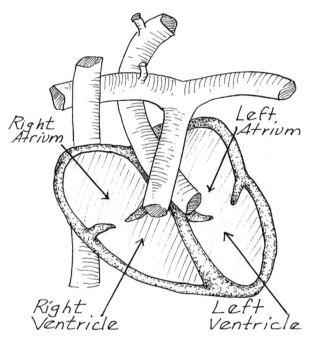

Hand out the Cardiovascular System Worksheet and proceed to work with small groups of students on some of the adaptations. Also, if time permits, have the students participate in the Whole Class Lab at the end of this activity.

Cardiovascular System

Choose the correct answer to the following questions.

1. The cardiovascular system:
   a. carries nutrients and oxygen to your cells
   b. transports disease-fighting cells to internal organs of the body
   c. removes the waste from your cells
   d. does all of the above

2. An average heart is approximately the size of:
   a. your fist
   b. your palm
   c. a cantaloupe
   d. a football

3. Waste leaves the blood through the body as:
   a. oxygen
   b. glucose
   c. carbon dioxide
   d. water

4. The heart is divided into two parts by the:
   a. ventricles
   b. septum
   c. sternum
   d. atrium

5. The lower chambers of the heart are called the:
   a. sternum
   b. ventricles
   c. atria
   d. vessels

6. The top chambers of the heart are called the:
   a. atria
   b. vessels
   c. ventricles
   d. sternum

7. When blood leaves the heart from the ventricles, it first travels through the:
   a. veins
   b. arteries
   c. ventricles
   d. atria

8. The blood vessels that bring the blood back to the heart are called the:
   a. arteries
   b. veins
   c. chambers
   d. sternum

How to Adapt This Lesson for the Inclusive Classroom
For Learning Disabled Students

Write the following terms on one side of a set of note cards, using a different colored marker for each term:

glucose	sternum	chambers
carbon dioxide	circulatory	arteries
ventricle	cardiovascular	veins
atrium	vessels	

Write the definition of each of these terms on the opposite side of the cards with the corresponding colored markers. These definitions can be discussed and obtained from class notes and a dictionary. Keep definitions short and simple so they are easy to remember. If students can think of a small picture to help remember a given definition, draw this on the note card with a colored marker. Students can also label a diagram of the heart.

Read a term or definition and ask students to identify or define the word. Continue in a game-like fashion until the students are more comfortable with the vocabulary. Then proceed to the worksheet.

For understanding how the heart functions, use the following strategy:

The ABCs of the Heart

A = Atrium takes the blood into the top chamber.

B = Blood goes into the ventricle.

C = Cardiovascular system carries blood away from the heart to the cells of the body through the arteries.

S = System carries blood to veins and back into the atrium of the heart, and the cycle repeats.

This strategy can be written on a flip chart so it is easy to see and discuss.

For Delayed Readers

If students have difficulties with the pronunciation of unfamiliar terms, reteach and rewrite words phonetically on the worksheet. Read each question aloud, asking students to paraphrase the question. Discuss possible answers to a given question, encouraging students to visualize what the question is asking them. Go through all possible multiple choice answers. Lead students to the correct answer, having them close their eyes to visualize why the answer is correct. Continue in this way with the remaining questions.

For Students with Behavioral Difficulties or ADD/ADHD

Group these students with those who have reading or learning concerns, and allow them to review the note cards and strategies to strengthen their understanding. Empowering these students in this interactive way can be a strong motivating tool for aiding focusing and work. These students can also either jot down or mentally answer the questions before looking at the provided answers, because the multiple choice format can sometimes be confusing.

For Gifted Learners

Expand on this lesson by having gifted learners research various types of heart diseases and prevention methods, which they can orally present to the class.

Whole Class Lab: Blood Cell Boogie

Purpose: Students will understand how blood cells travel through the body.
    This lab works best with groups of five students.

Supplies

transparency of relay course

Supplies (per group)

five inflated red balloons

five inflated blue balloons

poster or drawing of the lungs

playground chalk or masking tape

1. Set up the relay course (a huge diagram of the heart) ahead of time in a gymnasium or on the playground (see the diagram that follows). If you are using a gymnasium, mark off the parts of the circulatory system with masking tape. If using the playground, mark them off with playground chalk.

2. Prior to beginning the lab, review the parts of the circulatory system with the students.

3. Show the students the relay course and review the circulatory pathway. You may wish to use a transparency of the course to enhance your explanation.

4. Divide the students into teams. Explain to students that the red balloons will represent oxygenated blood cells, and the blue balloons will represent carbon dioxide–loaded blood cells that have given away their oxygen and are now carrying away the cells' waste.

5. Illustrate the path with the help of one student volunteer. Walk the student slowly through this pathway:

    a. Students begin in the left ventricle as oxygenated blood cells (each carrying a red balloon).

    b. They travel through the aorta.

    c. After passing through the aorta, students carry their oxygenated blood cells to the muscles.

    d. From the muscles, students carry carbon dioxide–loaded blood (blue balloons) to the right atrium.

    e. From the right atrium, students travel into the right ventricle.

    f. Students travel through the pulmonary artery.

g. From the pulmonary artery, students travel into the lungs, where they exchange their carbon dioxide for oxygen (exchanging blue for red balloons).

h. Now carrying oxygenated blood, students enter the left atrium and are ready to begin the circulatory cycle again.

6. Have one group of five students start the process. One student must go through the entire circulatory system before the next student blood cell may continue. Have a member of the group act as the timer and begin timing with a stopwatch, with the first student starting from the left ventricle, and end timing when the last student reenters the left atrium from the heart. Have another member of the group act as the caller, directing the members going through the course. If each blood cell only takes twenty seconds to complete the circuit, a group should be able to complete the process in about one minute and forty seconds. Keep a record of group times to see which group circulates through the system most time efficiently.

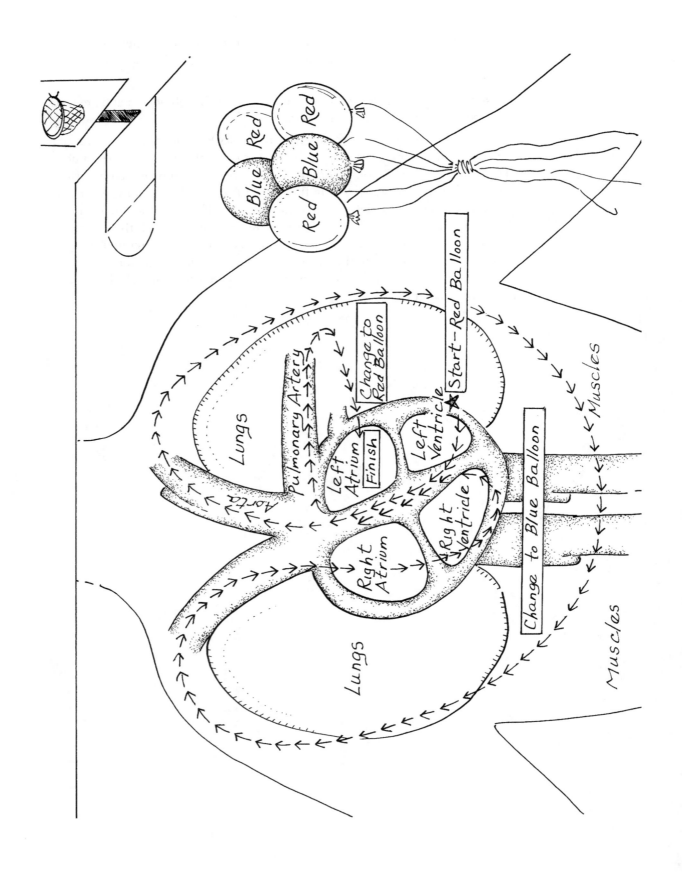

How to Adapt This Lab for the Inclusive Classroom
For Students with Physical Disabilities
If the course is too difficult for these students to navigate, allow them to fill the rolls of timer, who times their group, or caller, who helps direct the team.

Home/School Connection
Give students the following assignment to complete at home:

> Research ways to live a "heart-healthy" lifestyle; make a poster that explains how the heart works and how the things you discovered in your research help keep the heart healthy. Bring your poster to class to display.

How to Evaluate This Lesson
If time permits, we recommend an interview format. With individual students, discuss how the heart works, as well as how to prevent heart disease and live a heart-healthy lifestyle. Give students the topic of discussion before the assessment to aid in their preparation and review. You could also do a partner interview, with two students at a time.

Activity 3: The Central Nervous System

Purpose: Students will understand the functions of the central nervous system and how this system interacts with other body systems.

Read through the lesson and the adaptations and make sure you have the supplies you will need.

Supplies for the main lesson

chalkboard, overhead projector, computer with presentation software, or interactive whiteboard

science notebooks

Supplies for the adaptations

diagram of the brain and spinal cord

colored markers

Lesson

1. Begin by saying something like, "Today we are going to talk about the central nervous system. What can anyone tell me about it?" Lead a class discussion.

2. When the discussion is finished, write the following definition on the board and have students take notes in their notebooks:

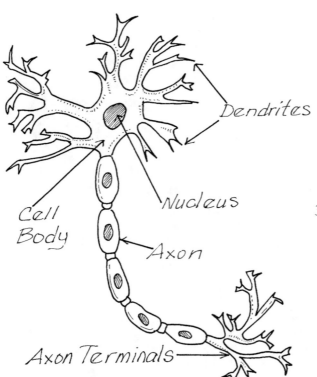

Dendrites

Nucleus

Cell Body

Axon

Axon Terminals

The Central Nervous System: The central nervous system consists of the brain and the spinal cord. The nerves branching off of the brain and spinal cord make up the peripheral nervous system. These systems work together to tell the brain what is happening inside and outside of the body. The central nervous system also makes sure that the body responds appropriately to the messages sent. This taking in and reporting of information within the central nervous system is called homeostasis.

3. Explain that the nervous system is made up of special cells, which are called *neurons,* and that each neuron contains dendrites and axons. Write the following definitions on the board for students to copy down in their notebooks.

   a. **Axons:** Axons carry impulses (information) away from the neuron.

   b. **Dendrites:** These carry nerve impulses to the neuron.

Differentiated Instruction for the Middle School Science Teacher

Then say, "An impulse reaches the tip of an axon and jumps to another via an electrical impulse at the synapse. The axon then releases a chemical that allows the impulse to cross the synapse to the next neuron. This is how messages travel through the central nervous system."

4. Brainstorm with the class to come up with examples in which a message is instantly received by the brain, and the body appropriately reacts to the stimulus. (Some examples might include putting your hand on a hot stove, touching very cold water, and so on.)

5. Now talk about the brain as part of the central nervous system: "The brain is the main information center of the body. Messages travel to the brain through the synapses of neurons in the central nervous system. The brain then interprets this information and allows the body to act upon it.

6. Describe the three main parts of the brain: the cerebrum, the cerebellum, and the brain stem:

   a. **The Cerebrum:** The cerebrum is the largest area of the brain. It is found at the front of the brain and is divided into a right and left half, or hemisphere. Its functions include learning, interpreting information, logical reasoning, abstract thought, speech and language, vision, interpreting the senses, and memory.

   b. **The Cerebellum:** The cerebellum is the second largest area of the brain and controls voluntary muscle movement and balance.

   c. **The Brain Stem:** The brain stem (also called Medulla), which is found between the spinal cord and cerebellum, controls all of your body's involuntary actions. Examples of brain stem activity include your heartbeat, breathing, and salivating.

Cerebrum

Cerebellum

Medulla (Brain Stem)

Hand out the Central Nervous System Worksheet and proceed to work with small groups of students on some of the adaptations. Also, if time permits, have the students participate in the Whole Class Lab at the end of this activity.

Central Nervous System Worksheet

Fill in the blanks with the answers that best complete the sentences.

1. The brain and the spinal cord make up the: _____.

2. Nerves branching off the brain and spinal cord make up the: _____.

3. Information from one neuron flows to another neuron across a _____, which contains a small gap separating neurons.

4. _____ carry impulses to the neuron.

5. _____ carry impulses away from the neuron.

6. There are _____ major parts of the brain.

7. The function of _____ is to make sure the body responds appropriately to various stimuli that enter the system.

8. The part of the brain that controls your heartbeat is called the: _____.

9. The part of the brain that controls movement and balance is called the: _____.

10. The largest part of the brain, which controls speaking, abstract thought, and many other higher-level functions, is called the: _____.

How to Adapt This Lesson for the Inclusive Classroom

For Learning Disabled Students

Make a word bank using the answers to the worksheet. These terms can be retaught and reviewed individually:

cerebrum	central nervous system	peripheral nervous system
cerebellum	synapse	axons
brain stem	dendrites	homeostasis
neurons		

For Students with Cognitive Difficulties

The function of the central nervous system is an abstract concept and sometimes difficult to grasp. Copy and pass out a diagram of the brain and spinal cord (see page 189). Have students color and label each section of the diagram and review. Hang these up in the classroom to reinforce the concepts.

For Delayed Readers

Break down words from the word bank phonetically and write them on word cards. Review words and definitions with students. Then ask students to read, write, and explain all terms included in the word bank.

For Resistant Learners or Students with ADD/ADHD

Empower students in an interactive way by pairing them with delayed readers or struggling students to review and discuss word bank terms and definitions.

For Gifted Learners

Expand on this lesson by having students develop a small skit or puppet show explaining the function of the central nervous system in a fun, easy-to-understand format.

Whole Class Lab: Are You Predominately a Right- or Left-Brain Thinker?

Purpose: Students will understand the various functions of the right and left hemispheres of the cerebrum.

This lab is best performed in pairs.

Supplies (per pair)

two copies of the checklist (below)

two pens

lined paper

1. Hand out copies of the checklist below and instruct students to check off which adjectives best describe themselves.

Checklist

_____ Uses logic to determine decisions

_____ Uses feeling to determine decisions

_____ Is detail oriented

_____ Is "big picture" oriented

_____ Is interested in facts

_____ Has a good imagination

_____ Uses words and language to navigate the world

_____ Enjoys symbols, images, and maps as ways to get around

_____ Is past and present oriented

_____ Is present and future oriented

_____ Loves math and science

_____ Loves philosophy, psychology, and religion

_____ Comprehends meaning and details; is studious

_____ Can "get it" quickly; uses information immediately

_____ Knows a lot of facts; knows object names

_____ Appreciates things; knows object functions

_____ Likes patterns, order

_____ Believes in things, self

_____ Is artistic; has good spatial perception

_____ Is mechanical; understands the strategies of how things work

_____ Is safe, practical, and reality based

_____ Enjoys fantasy; presents possibilities

Information in survey adapted from the research of Roger Sperry on cerebral hemispheres, from 1973 to the present.

2. Once students have completed the survey, read them the answers that correspond to the right or left brain (included in the answer key, page 223), so that each student may determine whether his or her main personality characteristics are right- or left-brain oriented.

3. Students should discuss the results with their lab partners and write half-page reactions about themselves and the results of the survey.

How to Adapt This Lab for the Inclusive Classroom

For Delayed Readers

Review the characteristics on the survey with these students, before they fill in the answers.

For Students with Cognitive Difficulties

Explain the survey items in simple terms that are easy to understand.

For Students with Fine Motor Difficulties

Allow students to outline their thoughts in a bulleted list, or offer the use of a scribe or a keyboard to complete the lab assignment.

Home/School Connection

Give students the following assignment to complete at home:

Cut a lemon in quarters with a knife. Pass a wedge to each family member. Tell each member to visualize eating the lemon. No one should actually eat the lemon. What happens? Take a survey of the results. Explain how this relates to brainstem activity and write a paragraph explaining your results. Bring your paragraph to class for discussion.

How to Evaluate This Lesson

We suggest you evaluate multiple aspects of student participation. A rubric may be used as follows:

Worksheet answers	40 percent
Class participation	15 percent
Lab results	25 percent
Home/School Connection	20 percent

Activity 4: The Digestive System

Purpose: Students will learn about the parts and functions of the digestive system.

Read through the lesson and the adaptations and make sure you have the supplies you will need.

Supplies for the main lesson

chalkboard, overhead projector, computer with presentation software, or interactive whiteboard

science notebooks

blender

banana

two chocolate cookies

½ cup of white vinegar

2 tablespoons of water

transparency diagram of the digestive system

Supplies for the adaptations

diagram of digestive system

handout with terms and definitions

Lesson

1. Begin by saying something like, "Today we are going to talk about digestion. Can anyone share what they know about digestion?" Facilitate a discussion of the digestive system.

2. When the discussion is completed, say, "There are two main types of digestion: mechanical and chemical digestion. These types work together to digest food and nourish all of the cells in the body."

3. Write the following definitions on the board for students to copy down in their notebooks:

   a. **Mechanical Digestion:** Mechanical digestion is the physical act of breaking down the food we eat. Chewing food into bite-size pieces and swallowing start the process of mechanical digestion. Digestion continues as the food moves from the esophagus to the stomach and to the small and large intestines. It is completed when the food travels into the bloodstream as nutrients or is eliminated as waste.

   b. **Chemical Digestion:** Chemical digestion occurs when food is broken down chemically by acids in the stomach and changes into nutrients and sugars that the body needs in order to survive.

4. Demonstrate each concept with the following activity:

   a. Put the banana and cookies in the blender and pulse until the food is broken up into bite-size pieces. This demonstrates mechanical digestion.

   b. Add the vinegar and water and blend. The acid in the vinegar changes the appearance of the food and breaks it down into a frothy liquid. This is similar to what happens during chemical digestion.

5. Then describe the process of digestion orally, while showing it on an overhead transparency:

a. Digestion begins when food enters the mouth. Bite-size pieces of food are broken down in the mouth by enzymes (proteins that increase the rate of chemical reactions) found in the saliva.

b. The food then moves down a long tube called the esophagus. Food is pushed into the stomach by an expanding and contracting process known as peristalsis.

c. The food then enters the stomach. The stomach churns the food until it resembles a thick liquid.

d. Next the food enters the small intestine, where enzymes and acids are secreted. These enzymes and acids are made in the liver, small intestine, and pancreas. All food is chemically digested during this phase.

e. Lastly, undigested food and waste goes to the large intestine, and the waste is eliminated. Nutrients enter the bloodstream to fuel all cells of the body. The process during which molecules enter the bloodstream, by passing from the small intestine to the large intestine through a semipermeable membrane, is called osmosis. The uptake of food (or other substances) from the digestive tract is called absorption.

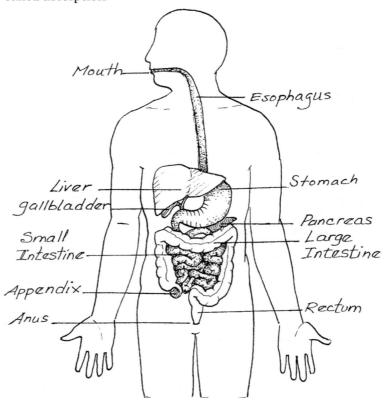

Hand out the Digestive System Worksheet and proceed to work with small groups of students on some of the adaptations. Also, if time permits, have the students participate in the Whole Class Lab at the end of this activity.

Digestive System Worksheet

Unscramble the following words and write a short-answer definition for each item.

1. SSEPRITALIS:

   _____

   _____

   _____

2. CAPNREAS:

   _____

   _____

   _____

3. UGOSEPHAS:

   _____

   _____

   _____

4. ROSBAPTION:

   _____

   _____

   _____

5. MOTSACH:

   _____

   _____

   _____

6. Briefly explain the process of digestion.

   _____

   _____

   _____

   _____

   _____

How to Adapt This Lesson for the Inclusive Classroom

For Learning Disabled Students

Students may take notes on a graphic organizer or label a diagram of the digestive system. Students with learning difficulties can use the following mnemonic to remember the steps of the digestive process:

The MESS Strategy

M = Mouth. Mechanical and chemical digestion occurs here. Food is chewed and mixed with saliva.

E = Esophagus. The food travels down the esophagus into the stomach when muscles in the esophagus contract and expand. This is called peristalsis.

S = Stomach. Food is pushed from the esophagus into the stomach, where it is mixed with gastric juices (liquids found in the stomach) and broken down into a liquid.

S = Small and Large Intestines. More digestive juices mix with the food when it reaches the small intestine, and the food is broken down into nutrient molecules. These nutrients enter the bloodstream through absorption and nourish all cells. The large intestine eliminates waste.

You can also aid students individually in unscrambling terms and finding definitions within the class notes.

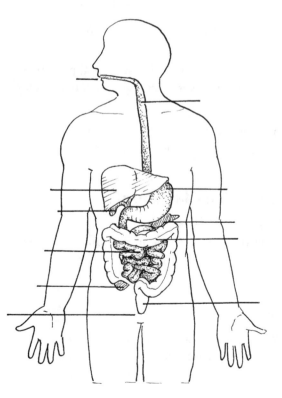

For Delayed Readers or Students with Memory Weaknesses

Develop a graphic organizer to visually represent the main points of the digestive process.

For Students with Fine Motor or Perceptual Difficulties

Type the definitions of terms and give them to these students to reduce writing time in class. Students can also label diagrams rather than write out definitions.

For Gifted Learners

Expand on this lesson by having students develop a board game based on the digestive process. When they have completed the game, students can teach the class how to play.

For Resistant Learners or Students with ADD/ADHD

Behaviorally challenged students enjoy lessons that are fast paced and interactive. Have each of these students pair with a stronger student and write a rap or jingle explaining the digestive process; then have them present their songs to the class.

Whole Class Lab: What Is Osmosis and What Role Does It Play in Digestion?

Purpose: Students will understand that digestion turns solid foods into liquid, which are then able to pass through the intestine walls into the bloodstream through the process of osmosis.

This lab works best with groups of four students.

Supplies (per group)

1 teaspoon of red food coloring

tall drinking glass ½ filled with water

celery stalk with leaves

piece of masking tape

marker

1. Have students add food coloring to their glasses of water.

2. Each group then stands the celery stalk in the glass near a sunny window. Using a marker, each lab group should put their names on a piece of tape to mark the glass.

3. Have students leave the celery stalks to sit in the glasses overnight.

4. The next day, ask students to observe what has occurred.

5. Write the following definitions of osmosis and absorption on the board:

   a. **Osmosis:** Osmosis is the process during which liquids move through a membrane.

   b. **Absorption:** During absorption, the nutrients from digested food pass into the blood vessels in the wall of the intestine. Osmosis is one mechanism for absorption.

Students should write a one-paragraph description of how this experiment explains the processes of osmosis and absorption. Have them relate their answers to the digestive process covered in class.

How to Adapt This Lab for the Inclusive Classroom
For Students with Fine Motor or Perceptual Difficulties

Allow these students to use the keyboard to write, or have them orally explain to you the results of the experiment in an interview format.

Home/School Connection

Give students the following assignment to complete at home:

Design a brochure, similar to those found in a doctor's office, explaining the process of digestion. Use illustrations, diagrams, and facts to attractively present this topic to the reader. Bring your brochure into class.

How to Evaluate This Lesson

We recommend a traditional assessment to evaluate students' understanding of the digestive system. Dictate several key vocabulary words and ask students to write short definitions on lined paper. Also, ask students to briefly explain the digestive process. Factor the quiz, worksheet, Home/School Connection, and lab participation into the final grade, as follows:

Quiz	60 percent
Worksheet	15 percent
Lab	10 percent
Home/School Connection	15 percent

Activity 5: Blood

Purpose: Students will understand the parts and functions of blood, and will learn about the four major blood types and some blood diseases.

Read through the lesson and the adaptations and make sure you have the supplies you will need.

Supplies for the main lesson

chalkboard, overhead projector, computer with presentation software, or interactive whiteboard

science notebooks

Supplies for the adaptations

note cards

assorted colored markers

four 4- to 6-inch Styrofoam disks

twelve large red gumdrops

twelve green gumdrops

box of toothpicks

Lesson

1. Begin the lesson by asking students if anyone knows the four major blood types and what his or her own blood type is. Tell the students that they are going to learn about the types and functions of blood in today's lesson.

2. Write the following definitions of blood parts and their functions on the board and have students take notes:

    a. **Plasma:** Plasma is made up mostly of water. It carries nutrients, vitamins, and minerals to all cells. It also carries waste products away from the cells to be eliminated from the body. Plasma is yellow. There are three main groups of plasma proteins. One group regulates how much water there is in the blood. Another group helps fight diseases. The third group of plasma proteins works with platelets, helping the blood to clot.

    b. **Red Blood Cells:** Red blood cells are made in your bone marrow. Without red blood cells, your body cannot use oxygen. Because there are no nuclei in red blood cells, they cannot reproduce themselves. They rely solely on bone marrow to make new cells. Red blood cells have a life span of only 120 days.

    c. **White Blood Cells:** White blood cells are also made in the bone marrow. White blood cells are important because they fight disease. As soon as bacteria enter the body, some of the white blood cells near the site notify the others for help. Many cells travel to the site to fight the bacteria or disease. White blood cells are much bigger than red blood cells. They have nuclei and can reproduce themselves. They live for months or years.

d. **Platelets:** Platelets are parts of cells that look like fibers. They help to form blood clots when cuts or wounds occur. When a cut or wound occurs, platelets surround the area and release a substance called fibrin. Fibrin produces fibers that act like a net to stop blood loss.

3. Next talk about the four major blood types: A, B, AB, and O. Explain that blood types are determined by markers. Then say, "Markers are proteins that are on the red blood cells. They are arranged differently for each blood type. This is how scientists and doctors can determine the type of blood you have. This is very important information if you need a blood transfusion. A blood transfusion occurs when a person receives blood intravenously because his or her body has suffered a loss of blood due to accident, trauma, or disease. To have a safe transfusion, the blood must be properly cared for in a hospital or blood bank, be administered properly to the patient, and be the correct blood type.

"Certain blood types can mix only with other specific types. This is because the body can recognize the markers of its particular blood type. O has no A or B markers, so it can be donated and recognized by both A and B. Blood type O can be donated to all blood types, and blood type AB can receive all blood types." The following may be written on the board for clarification.

Blood type A can only mix with types A and O.

Blood type B can only mix with B and O.

Blood type AB can mix with A, B, AB, and O.

Blood type O can receive O only.

4. Finally, introduce some common blood diseases:

a. **Sickle Cell Anemia:** This disease occurs when red blood cells are in the shape of a sickle or a crescent. Because of this shape, blood cells are not flexible and don't travel to all parts of the body very well. Cells then become deprived of oxygen that they need to survive. People can become very tired, short of breath, and sick with this disease. Sickle cell anemia is an inherited disease.

b. **Hemophilia:** Hemophilia is a disease that affects the blood clotting process. It manifests itself in a breakdown in the organization of blood clotting.

c. **Leukemia:** This disease is a form of cancer that involves white blood cells and bone marrow. In a person with leukemia, an abnormal amount of white blood cells is produced. These cells take the space needed for normal red blood cell growth to occur. This abnormal blood production can be fatal over time.

Hand out the Blood Worksheet and proceed to work with small groups of students on some of the adaptations. Also, if time permits, have the students participate in the Whole Class Lab at the end of this activity.

Name: _____   Date: _____

Blood Worksheet

Unscramble the following words and write the definitions in the blanks provided.

1. SLPAMA:

   _____

   _____

   _____

2. LLPATEETS:

   _____

   _____

   _____

3. DER OBLOD ECLLS:

   _____

   _____

   _____

4. PMHEOHILAI:

   _____

   _____

   _____

5. RMAKERS:

   _____

   _____

   _____

6. LBODO PTYE:

   _____

   _____

   _____

7. ODNOR:

   _____

   _____

   _____

8. OFRTANSUSIN:

   _____

   _____

   _____

How to Adapt This Lesson for the Inclusive Classroom

For Learning Disabled Students

Provide students with the words already unscrambled and assist them in reviewing and rewriting definitions in their simplest forms. Using colored markers, students can write terms and definitions on the front and back of note cards.

For Students with Cognitive Difficulties

These students often struggle with abstract concepts, and can benefit from visual and tactile examples. Make the following models of the four major blood types and display them in the classroom:

Blood Type Marker Models

1. Insert toothpicks into four red gumdrops. Press the toothpicks evenly into the side of the first Styrofoam disk. Label the disk Blood Type Marker A.

2. Repeat the same process with the green gumdrops for Blood Type Marker B.

3. Insert toothpicks into the remaining red and green gumdrops. Alternating red and green gumdrops, evenly insert the toothpicks into the side of the third disk. Label this disk Blood Type Marker AB.

4. Label the last disk Blood Type Marker O. This disk does not have any gumdrops.

Show students the models while explaining the facts about blood types from the lesson.

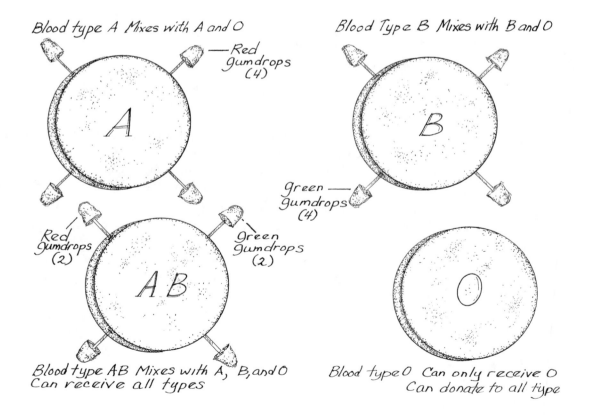

Blood type A Mixes with A and O — Red gumdrops (4)

Blood Type B Mixes with B and O

green Gumdrops (4)

Red Gumdrops (2)   green Gumdrops (2)

Blood type AB Mixes with A, B, and O Can receive all types

Blood type O Can only receive O Can donate to all type

For Students with Visual, Motor, or Perceptual Difficulties

Provide these students with printed copies of notes from this lesson to put into their notebooks. They may also use wide-ruled paper or a computer keyboard to write the definitions for the worksheet questions.

For Delayed Readers

Unscramble the words on the worksheet to avoid confusion. Read aloud the notes with students to asses their reading fluency and understanding of the definitions. Highlight the new and difficult vocabulary words. Discuss simple definitions and word usage with the students. Reread the notes and worksheet terms aloud.

For Gifted Learners

Have these students research the process of donating blood. Students can then inform the class through a PowerPoint presentation about the importance of blood drives, uses of blood, positive and negative factors of donating, who are good candidates to give blood, and where blood is given. After the presentation, students can engage the class in a discussion about who might be interested in donating blood in the future.

Whole Class Lab: Blood Types

Purpose: This lab shows how blood types are compatible.

This lab works best with groups of three or four students.

Supplies (per group)

four 6- to 8-ounce clear plastic tumblers

black markers

red and yellow food coloring

four plastic spoons

1. Each group should use markers to label the tumblers A, B, AB, and O.
2. They then fill each tumbler ¾ full with water.
3. Each group should place 2 drops of red food coloring in tumbler A, 2 drops of yellow food coloring in tumbler B, and 1 drop each of red and yellow food coloring in tumbler AB. Tumbler O has only water. Remind them to stir each mixture with a separate, clean spoon, and to rinse off spoons when finished.
4. Students should place 2 teaspoons of red liquid from tumbler A in each of the other cups and stir. They should note if any change occurs in any of the mixtures. Have students fill out copies of the following chart by checking if there is a change in color in any of the mixtures. Have them repeat this process with the remaining cups. After they have filled out the chart, students should answer the questions that follow.

	Type A	Type B	Type AB	Type O
Type A	•••			
Type B		•••		
Type AB			•••	
Type O				•••

1. What happened when you added type A mixture to type B?

_____

_____

2. What happened to the color when you added type A mixture to type AB?

_____

_____

3. What happened to type O mixture when you added it to type A?

_____

_____

4. Based on charting the changes that have occurred, what can your group conclude? Use your class notes as a reference.

_____

_____

_____

_____

_____

_____

How to Adapt This Lab for the Inclusive Classroom

For Students with Visual, Motor, or Perceptual Difficulties

Help students fill the cups, add food coloring, or stir solutions. If writing is very difficult, assign another student to fill out the lab questions and chart.

For Students with Physical Disabilities

For the wheelchair-bound student, place a cutting board over the top of the wheelchair to give him or her a more secure surface on which to work with the lab supplies.

Home/School Connection

Have students complete the following assignment at home:

> With a family member, create a diagram, song, poem, or memory device to help remember the components and functions of blood.

How to Evaluate This Lesson

We suggest a traditional assessment for this activity. Quiz students on their understanding of the terms and concepts presented in the lesson. Consider grading as follows:

Quiz	35 percent
Worksheet	20 percent
Class participation	20 percent
Lab assignment	25 percent

Activity 6: The Ear

Purpose: Students will learn about the structure and function of the ear and some common diseases of the ear.

Read through the lesson and the adaptations and make sure you have the supplies you will need.

Supplies for the main lesson

chalkboard, overhead projector, computer with presentation software, or interactive whiteboard

megaphone

science notebooks

Supplies for the adaptations

note cards

assorted colored markers

construction paper

roll of paper towels for blindfolds

Lesson

1. Using a megaphone, tell the students, "Today the class will study the ear." Tell students that the outer ear takes in sounds and carries them to the brain, and that the megaphone takes sound waves and projects them outward. Discuss similarities between the ways the ear and the megaphone work.

2. Tell the students that there are three major regions of the ear, which are all designed to receive sound waves. Write the following on the board and have students take notes in their notebooks:

   a. **The Outer Ear:** This is the widest area of the funnel and is designed to gather sound waves. Sound enters the outer ear and travels to the eardrum.

   b. **The Middle Ear:** The tympanic membrane, commonly known as the eardrum, picks up the vibrations from the outer ear. Sound waves hit and vibrate the tympanic membrane, similar to the way a drum vibrates when it's hit. In the middle ear, there are three tiny, interconnected bones called the hammer, anvil, and stirrup. These bones help to transmit and amplify sounds by moving at the same frequency as the sound waves.

   c. **The Inner Ear:** The inner ear is made up of the cochlea, semicircular canal, and auditory nerve. The vibrations from the middle ear continue to travel in the fluid in the cochlea, which is a small, spiral tube that catches the sound. When the cochlear fluid vibrates, the neurons in the inner ear send nerve impulses to the brain. This happens through the auditory nerve. These impulses are the sounds that you hear. The semicircular canal is not involved with the hearing process at all. It aids in balance.

3. Next, talk about decibels (dB), saying, "Loudness is measured in units that are called decibels. They describe the force with which sound waves hit against the ear. Silence would be zero decibels. With every ten-decibel increase, the sound is intensified ten times. The chart shows the decibel level and intensity of some typical sounds.

Decibels Chart

Sound	Decibels	Intensity
Pin Dropping	10 dB	100
Watch Ticking	20 dB	200
Talking	60 dB	600
Alarm Clock	80 dB	800
Rock Concert	120 dB	1,200
Jet Plane	130 dB	1,300

4. Now talk about some common diseases of the ear.

a. **Conductive Hearing Loss:** Conductive hearing loss occurs when sound vibrations from the tympanic membrane to the inner ear are blocked. This can be caused by fluid in the middle ear, ear infections, abnormal bone growth, or earwax. The sound messages cannot get to the auditory nerve because of the blockage, and messages cannot get to the brain. Hearing is usually restored once the problem is corrected.

b. **Sensorineural Hearing Loss:** This disease occurs when there is damage to the auditory nerve. It is usually caused by traumatic injury, high blood pressure, or a birth defect. Hearing is not usually restored.

c. **Presbycusis:** This hearing loss usually occurs because of changes in the inner ear. This happens very gradually in the elderly. Hearing is usually not restored.

d. **Tinnitus:** Tinnitus is ringing in the ears. Reasons include ear infections and earwax. Once the problem is solved, hearing is usually restored.

Hand out the Ear Worksheet and proceed to work with small groups of students on some of the adaptations. Also, if time permits, have the students participate in the Whole Class Lab at the end of this activity.

Name: _____   Date: _____

Ear Worksheet

Answer each question by circling the answer that best completes the sentence.

1. The outer ear is designed to:
   a. amplify sound waves
   b. transmit sound waves to the auditory nerve
   c. collect sound waves
   d. do both a and c

2. Decibels measure:
   a. the frequency of sound
   b. hearing loss
   c. the intensity of sound
   d. auditory nerve function

3. The tympanic membrane is part of the:
   a. semicircular canal
   b. inner ear

   c. cochlear fluid
   d. middle ear

4. The three interconnected bones of the middle ear are called the:
   a. hammer, screw, and stirrup
   b. hammer, advil, and stirrup
   c. hammer, anvil, and stirrup
   d. hangar, anvil, and stirrup

5. The main job of the inner ear is to:
   a. send vibrations to the auditory nerve
   b. collect sounds that travel to the tympanic membrane
   c. pick up vibrations from the outer ear
   d. restore a sense of balance

Define the following terms in complete sentences.

6. Decibels:
   _____
   _____
   _____

7. Sensorineural hearing loss:
   _____
   _____
   _____

8. Conductive hearing loss:
   _____
   _____
   _____

9. In your own words, explain in detail how we hear sounds.
   _____
   _____
   _____
   _____
   _____
   _____
   _____
   _____

How to Adapt This Lesson for the Inclusive Classroom
For Learning Disabled Students
Read the items on the worksheet and review each multiple choice answer, covering up all other answers with a sheet of construction paper. Each possible choice can be discussed separately. Students should justify their final answers with documentation from the class notes, confirming and reinforcing answers before moving on to the next question.

For Students with Memory Weaknesses
Students with short-term memory weaknesses may find it difficult to explain how we hear sounds. Try the following mnemonic as a study device;

Sara's Trained Ears (helped her) Play the Saxophone and Violin Beautifully.

Sara's	= Sound enters the outer ear.
Trained	= Travels to the eardrum.
Ears	= Eardrum vibrates.
Play	= Passing vibrations travel into the middle ear.
Saxophone	= Sound passes through three small bones in the middle ear and travels to the inner ear.
Violin	= Vibrations occur in the inner ear fluid.
Beautifully	= Brain receives sound signals from the auditory nerve. We can then hear and interpret sounds!

Also, use class notes to fill in further details based on students' mastery of the information.

For Students with Perceptual Difficulties
Help students arrange the information provided in the mnemonic in a graphic organizer to give a visual representation of how sound travels.

For Resistant Learners or Students with ADD/ADHD
Pair the student who struggles with attending with a stronger student, and have them review the mnemonic and notes on the ear together.

For Gifted Learners
Expand on this lesson by having gifted learners design a game similar to the traditional Marco Polo to play with the whole class. Students can research intensities of sounds and find examples of about ten items, having a range from high to low decibels. The class will then divide into four to six teams. One student from each team is blindfolded. Gifted learners will play each sound individually in various parts of the room. The blindfolded students from each team will have to determine what the sound is and where it is coming from. Each team will get a point for correctly guessed items. The intensity can be altered each time. When items are answered correctly, the next team member will get a turn. The team with the most points wins.

Whole Class Lab: Organized Sound

Purpose: This lab will show how sound waves create different sounds based on the amount of water in a glass.

This experiment works best with groups of four to six students.

Supplies (per group)

three 8-ounce clear glass drinking cups (or glass mason jars)

water

three colors of food coloring

metal fork

two note cards

markers

1. Each group pours water into one glass until it's about ⅓ full. They then place a drop of one color of food coloring into the glass and stir.

2. Each group repeats the process with the second glass, this time filling the glass ½ full with water and choosing a second color to tint the water in this glass.

3. Lastly, groups fill their third glasses to the top and tint with the last color.

4. Using their forks, groups should lightly tap the top of each glass and take note of the sounds. They should notice that each sound is different. If necessary, groups should adjust the water until the sounds are distinctly different in each of their three glasses.

5. Have each group label the cups 1, 2, and 3. Each group then adjusts the sounds to make up a melody or song using the three notes that they have created.

6. Have groups write their songs on note cards, using the numbers to represent the order of the sounds. They then present their finished songs to the class.

7. After their presentations, groups should collaborate to write conclusions to this lab, recording their thoughts about how sound changes to discuss in class.

How to Adapt This Lab for the Inclusive Classroom
For Students with Fine Motor or Perceptual Difficulties

Use glass mason jars for more stability, so these students can easily participate in the lab. Drinking glasses may be too delicate.

For Resistant Learners or Students with ADD/ADHD

Group these learners with stronger students. Give assistance and extra supervision when students are tapping the glasses or jars with forks for sound.

For Students with Physical Disabilities

For the wheelchair-bound student, place a cutting board over the wheelchair to create a safe work surface. Assign a student or paraprofessional to give assistance when tapping glasses. Use mason jars rather than drinking glasses, for the sake of stability.

Home/School Connection

Have students complete the following assignment at home:

> Choose one topic about the ear covered in class that you found interesting, and research to find out more about that topic. Present the information by making an informative brochure on this topic, similar to those you would find in a doctor's office. Bring your brochure into class.

How to Evaluate This Lesson

If time permits, evaluate this lesson by interviewing students. Have a private dialogue with each student to talk about his or her understanding of the concepts, participation, lab work, Home/School Connection, and worksheet. Jointly decide on his or her level of understanding and mastery attained for this activity.

Activity 7: The Eye

Purpose: Students will understand the parts of the eye and how they work, and will explore some common vision problems. Students will also learn more about light and the color spectrum.

Read through the lesson and the adaptations and make sure you have the supplies you will need.

Supplies for the main lesson

chalkboard, overhead projector, computer with presentation software, or interactive whiteboard

science notebooks

prism

Supplies for the adaptations

note cards

construction paper

colored pencils

Internet access

Lesson

1. Ask the students if they can name the colors of the rainbow. Generate a discussion about the colors of the visible spectrum.

2. End the discussion by presenting the standard mnemonic for remembering the colors:

   Roy G. Biv
   R = Red
   O = Orange
   Y = Yellow
   G = Green
   B = Blue
   I = Indigo
   V = Violet

3. If it's a sunny day, show them a prism. Talk about how when the light passes through the prism, it splits up, and rays with different wavelengths bend in different directions, appearing to us as the colors of the visible spectrum.

4. Tell the students that this is all possible to see because of our vision. Explain that vision is the interpretation of light by the brain, and that vision has been said to be our most precious sense. Ask the students their opinions about this, generating further discussion.

5. Then say, "Humans use the sense of sight to interpret much of the world. However, we only see a very small part of the electromagnetic spectrum. Light is measured in nanometers. Our vision ranges from 380 to 760 nanometers. This is the visible spectrum. It ranges from very dark purple at 360 nanometers to near infrared at over 700 nanometers."

6. Describe how the eye works.

   a. Light enters the eye by striking the cornea, or outer shield on the eye. The light then passes to the pupil, the black dot in the center of the eye. The iris controls how much light enters the pupil. Irises are the colored parts of the eyes. The iris changes the size of the pupil based on how much light is present. The pupil becomes smaller on a bright, sunny day, and larger in the dark.

   b. From the pupil, the light goes to the lens. Light bends when it hits the lens. The image then turns upside down. This is similar to the process that occurs in a camera. The muscles on the side of the pupils adjust so the image is in focus.

   c. Light rays pass through the lens and hit the retina. Receptor cells called rods and cones interpret the image. Rod cells work best in the dark or in very dim light. They see mostly shades of black, white, and gray. Cone receptor cells interpret colors and work best in the sunlight.

   d. When light hits the rods and cones, images travel to the brain through the optic nerve. One image comes from the right eye, and the other from the left eye. When the information arrives at the brain, the image is interpreted right side up, and the images from both eyes are combined into one.

7. Explain that we have two eyes so that we can have depth perception. Say, "Depth perception is the ability to judge how near or far objects are in relation to one another. For example, keen depth perception is required to hit a baseball. In order to accurately hit the ball, you need to know how near or far the ball is in relation to the bat."

8. Discuss some common problems with vision:

   a. **Nearsightedness:** People with nearsightedness have difficulty seeing objects that are faraway, but they are able to see close-up objects clearly. Light has to travel extra lengths to reach the retina. The extra lengths cause objects to focus in front of the retina, or near it. Concave lenses, which can be in the form of glasses or contact lenses, and which bend the light before it reaches the retina, help the problem.

   b. **Farsightedness:** People who are farsighted can see faraway items very clearly, but things close up are blurry. The lens of the eye bends

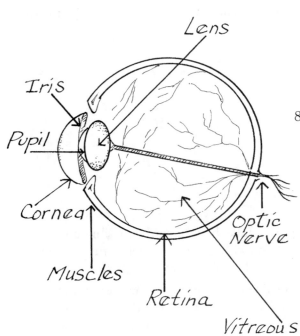

light such that images focus behind the retina. Convex lenses are thick in the middle, so light bends inward before reaching the eye. Because of this shift, the images focus on the retina.

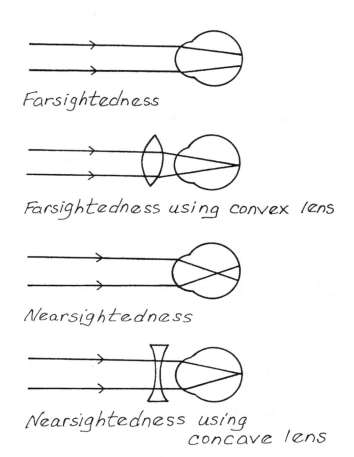

Hand out the Eye Worksheet and proceed to work with small groups of students on some of the adaptations. Also, if time permits, have the students participate in the Whole Class Lab at the end of this activity.

Eye Worksheet

Answer True or False to each statement.

1. _____ Vision is the interpretation of light by the optic nerve.

2. _____ Light separates when it goes through a prism because it has different wavelengths.

3. _____ The pupil is the colored part of the eye.

4. _____ Cone receptor cells in the eye interpret colors.

5. _____ Depth perception is the ability to judge when items are nearby.

6. _____ Concave lenses can correct the problem of nearsightedness.

7. _____ Rod cells best interpret shades of black, white, and gray.

8. _____ Convex lenses can correct the problem of farsightedness.

9. _____ The optic nerve sends images to the brain.

10. _____ The iris determines how much light enters the eye by making the pupil larger or smaller.

11. Briefly explain how we can see, in your own words.

_____

_____

_____

_____

_____

_____

How to Adapt This Lesson for the Inclusive Classroom
For Learning Disabled Students
Using the notes presented in class, help students answer the true-or-false questions in a small-group setting. One student can read an item aloud, while others peruse their notes and attempt to eliminate choices, until they determine the answer. Students may use construction paper to mask all other items.

Students can also play the game Who Wants to be an "Eye-n-stein"?

Who Wants to be an "Eye-n-Stein"?
1. Have small groups of learning disabled students divide into two teams, A and B.
2. Read each true-or-false question aloud. Allow team A to confer quietly or search their notes before giving the answer. If the answer is correct, the group receives a point. If not, Team B gets a turn with a new question.
3. Review all incorrectly answered questions at the end of the game.

For Students with Memory Weaknesses
Students with short-term memory weaknesses may find it difficult to explain how humans see. Try the following strategy as a study device:

See the LIGHT Strategy
L = Light enters the eye through the cornea.

I = Iris controls how much light enters the pupil.

G = Going from the pupil, the light bends to reach the lens.

H = Here the lens produces an upside-down image, similar to what occurs in a camera.

T = Traveling images go through the optic nerve to the brain.

Use class notes to fill in further details based on the students' mastery of the information. This information may also be put into a graphic organizer.

For Students with Cognitive Difficulties
The following terms may be difficult for some students to remember. Write each of them on one side of a note card. Have students draw pictures and write the definitions of the terms on the back of each card. Have students color the pictures, if time permits. When students are finished, use the deck of cards with the students to review.

cornea	iris	convex	pupil	nanometers	prism
optic nerve	concave	depth perception	nearsighted	farsighted	

For Students with ADD/ADHD
Use the game, mnemonic, and note cards presented above as focusing tools. Team these students with advanced students and have them review all class materials using the strategies. In this way, the learning will be fast paced, concise, and interactive.

For Gifted Learners

Expand on this lesson by having students create a PowerPoint presentation on "Magic Eye" images, which were very popular in the 1990s. Magic Eye images are three-dimensional images hidden within a two-dimensional pattern. Magic Eye images are a highly advanced form of stereogram, which is an optical illusion of depth created from flat, two-dimensional images. When an individual stares at one of these drawings for long enough, various images and depths are created. There are many sites online where students can research this topic, come up with examples, and further investigate the phenomena of depth perception. Have students present their findings and examples to the class.

Whole Class Lab: Is Vision Our Most Precious Sense?

Purpose: Students will experience what it would be like to lose their vision.

This experiment works best with students in pairs, and is best completed outdoors or in a wide, open space, such as a gym.

Supplies (per pair)

one blindfold (as dark as possible to prevent light from passing through)

1. One student in the pair is blindfolded.
2. The other student walks the blindfolded student around the space for five minutes, being a guide.
3. After five minutes, students stop and switch roles.
4. After the lab, have students answer and hand in the following essay question:

Explain your opinion of the walk. Would you support the statement that "Vision is our most precious sense"? Why or why not?

How to Adapt This Lab for the Inclusive Classroom
For Students with Physical Disabilities

If it is unsafe for a student with a physical disability to participate blindfolded, take the student in a less familiar area, such as a hallway or corridor, and ask him or her what he or she thinks might be there.

Home/School Connection

Have students complete the following assignment at home:

Interview family members to find out their beliefs regarding vision as their most precious sense. Then research two ways to take care of your eyes. Write these ways on a note card and bring them to class for a discussion.

How to Evaluate This Lesson

Evaluate this lesson with a short-answer quiz, asking students to explain how we see. Use the following percentages to grade students' work:

Quiz	40 percent
Lab	25 percent
Worksheet	15 percent
Home/School Connection	10 percent
Participation	10 percent

Answer Key

Chapter 5: Physical Science

Activity 1: Force

1. d
2. c
3. b
4. d
5. a
6. c
7. a
8. b

Activity 3: Properties of Matter

1. Mass—the amount of matter that is in an object
2. Weight—exent of gravitational pull to the earth
3. Volume—the amount of space occupied by a mass
4. Density—the amount of mass per unit volume of an object
5. Density equals mass divided by volume
6. Mass = density X volume
7. 2.7 g/cm^3
8. 6.0 g/cm^3
9. 0.60 g

Activity 4: Phases of Matter

1. melting point
2. melting point
3. freezing point
4. deposition
5. precipitation
6. vaporization
7. sublimation
8. evaporation
9. evaporation

Quiz

1. deposition
2. precipitation
3. water
4. gas changes to liquid
5. solid changes into gas
6. chocolate, crystals
7. liquid changes into gas

Activity 5: Acids and Bases

1. acid
2. base
3. base
4. acid
5. neutral
6. neutral
7. vinegar, orange juice, ascorbic acid, citric acid (Other answers may be accepted.)
8. soap, ammonia, detergents, lye (Other answers may be accepted.)

Activity 6: Using the Periodic Table

1. c
2. a
3. b
4. c
5. b
6. b
7. The element is carbon, the atomic number is 6, and the atomic mass is 12.011.

Activity 7: Alternative Energy Sources

1. A renewable resource is a natural resource that is depleted at a rate slower than the rate at which it regenerates.

2. Nonrenewable resources are those for which there are no ways to replenish the supply.

3. Examples of renewable resources include solar, wind, hydro-, and geothermal power.

4. Examples of nonrenewable resources include coal, petroleum, and natural gas.

5. Fossil fuels, also known as mineral fuels, are hydrocarbon-containing natural resources, such as coal, petroleum, and natural gas.

Chapter 6: Earth and Space Science

Activity 1: Types of Rocks

1. intrusive igneous rocks
2. granite
3. metamorphic rock
4. sedimentary rocks
5. igneous, sedimentary, and metamorphic
6. a. jewelry
   b. building stone
   c. filler in paint, plastics, and roofing cement
   d. monuments, statues, countertops, and floors
   e. curbing and countertops
   f. roads and foundations
   g. flooring and gravestones
   h. industrial and highway engineering
   i. scouring powder
   j. jewelry

Activity 2: Volcanoes

1. a
2. b
3. c

4. c
5. d
6. **Lava** Molten rock
7. **Gases** Carbon dioxide and sulfur dioxide. When mixed with lava and put under pressure, a volcanic explosion is created.
8. **Pyroclastic Materials** Rocks, glass fragments, and debris that come out of a volcano.

Activity 3: Minerals

1. a. False
   b. True
   c. False
   d. True
   e. False
2. naturally occurring, orderly crystalline structure, inorganic, definite chemical composition, solids
3. from magma, changes in temperature and pressure, precipitation, and hydrothermal solutions
4. color, luster, streak, crystal form, hardness, fracture, cleavage

Activity 4: Oceans and Seas

1. e
2. i
3. d
4. b
5. f
6. g
7. c
8. h
9. j
10. a

Activity 5: The Solar System

1. c
2. b
3. c

4. c
5. b
6. d
7. c
8. d
9. a
10. a

Activity 6: Stars and Galaxies

1. red
2. light-year
3. nuclear fusion
4. sun
5. Vega
6. spiral
7. interstellar matter
8. lenticular galaxies
9. Andromeda galaxy
10. galaxies

Activity 7: The Water Cycle

1. solid—ice, liquid—water, gas—evaporated water
2. a. Percolation-Movement of water through rocks and soil.
   b. Condensation-The process through which gas becomes a liquid
   c. Precipitation-Happens when the clouds become saturated, and excess moisture falls to the earth in the form of rain, freezing rain, snow, hail, or ice.
   d. The process through which water evaporates from plants

Chapter 7: Life Science

Activity 1: Classification of Organisms

1. Bacteria, Archaea, Eukarya
2. protists, plants, animals, fungi

3. (Several answers are possible. Here are just a few from the lesson.)
   Protists—seaweed
   Fungi—mushrooms, mold, mildew, yeast
   Plants—flowering plants, weeds, vegetables, trees
   Animals—dog
4. domain, kingdom, phylum, class, order, family, genus, species
5. Dog classification:
   Domain—Eukarya
   Kingdom—Animalia
   Phylum—Chordata
   Class—Mammalia
   Order—Carnivora
   Family—Canidae
   Genus—Canis Familaris (dog)
   Species—Lupus (dog)

Activity 2: The Structure and Function of Cells

1. d
2. g
3. f
4. e
5. i
6. h
7. b
8. a
9. j
10. k
11. c
12. cells are basic units of living things
    all living things are made of cells
    all cells come from other cells

Activity 3: Cell Division—Mitosis

1. Mitosis is the process in which cells split and divide to continue the growth and development of the organism.

2. Interphase. Here cells stay the longest to collect nutrients and gain strength.

3. The chromosomes condense and move to opposite sides of the nucleus.

4. Metaphase. Chromosomes line up in the middle of the cell.

5. In telephase, the chromosomes stretch out. A new nucleus is formed at each end of the cell. This houses divided chromosomes. The cell splits in the middle, forming two identical daughter cells, and the cycle repeats.

Activity 4: Cell Division—Meiosis

1. d
2. c
3. b
4. b

Activity 5: Heredity and Genetics

1. d
2. a
3. b
4. c
5a. Bb, Bb, Bb, Bb; 100 percent chance brown eyes (BB and Bb)
5b. XX, XY, XX, XY; 50 percent chance male, 50 percent chance female

Activity 6: Plants

1. **Nonvascular Plants** Plants that grow on the ground as a ground cover. Roots do not feed the rest of the plant structure by absorbing water.

   Vascular Plants Plants that have tubes in the roots, stems, and leaves that nourish them with food and water.

2. mosses, hornworts, liverworts
3. Tomatoes, sunflowers, lily
4. Have a vascular system and need pollen to reproduce.
5. Student's own words. No example here.

Chapter 8: The Human Body

Activity 1: The Skeletal System, Joints, and Muscles

1. True
2. False
3. True
4. False
5. True
6. True
7. True
8. False
9. True
10. True

Activity 2: The Cardiovascular System

1. d
2. a
3. c
4. b
5. b
6. a
7. b
8. b

Activity 3: The Central Nervous System

1. central nervous system
2. peripheral nervous system
3. synapse
4. dendrites
5. axons
6. three
7. homeostasis
8. brainstem
9. cerebellum
10. cerebrum

Activity 3: Whole Class Lab

_L_ Uses logic to determine decisions

_R_ Uses feeling to determine decisions

_L_ Is detail oriented

_R_ Is "big picture" oriented

_L_ Is interested in facts

_R_ Has a good imagination

_R_ Uses words and language to navigate the world

_L_ Enjoys symbols, images, and maps as ways to get around

_L_ Is past and present oriented

_R_ Is present and future oriented

_L_ Loves math and science

_R_ Loves philosophy, psychology, and religion

_L_ Comprehends meaning and details; is studious

_R_ Can "get it" quickly; uses information immediately

_L_ Knows a lot of facts; knows object names

_R_ Appreciates things; knows object functions

_L_ Likes patterns, order

_R_ Believes in things, self

_R_ Is artistic; has good spatial perception

_L_ Is mechanical; understands the strategies of how things work

_L_ Is safe, practical, and reality based

_R_ Enjoys fantasy; presents possibilities

Activity 4: The Digestive System

1. **Peristalsis** The process of food entering the stomach through expansion and contraction.

2. **Pancreas** An organ that aids digestion by making enzymes and acids, which chemically digest food.

3. **Esophagus** The passage where food moves from the throat to the stomach.

4. **Absorption** Process in digestion in which nutrients nourish all cells of the body.

5. **Stomach** A digestive organ in which food is mixed and partially digested.

Activity 5: Blood

1. **Plasma** A protein in the blood that carries nutrients, vitamins, and minerals to the cells.

2. **Platelets** Parts of blood cells that aid in clotting.

3. **Red Blood Cells** Blood cells made in the bone marrow that enable the body to use oxygen.

4. **Hemophilia** A blood disease that affects and alters the blood clotting process.

5. **Markers** Pieces of genetic material that identify particular characteristics in the blood.

6. **Blood Type** Name for a blood group. There are four main groups in the human body; A, AB, B and O.

7. **Donor** Blood given from one person that can be used in a tranfusion for another.

8. **Transfusion** The act of giving blood or blood parts to another person intravenously.

Activity 5: Whole Class Lab

1. yellow turned to orange

2. color deepened but did not change

3. mixture turned red

Activity 6: The Ear

1. c

2. c

3. d

4. c

5. a

6. **Decibels** Units that measure the loudness of sound.

7. **Sensorineural Hearing Loss** A disease that damages the auditory nerve to the point that hearing is not able to be restored.

8. **Conductive Hearing Loss** Hearing loss that occurs when the sound vibrations from the tympanic membrane to the inner ear are blocked.

Activity 7: The Eye

1.	False	6.	True
2.	True	7.	True
3.	False	8.	True
4.	True	9.	True
5.	True	10.	True

National Curriculum Standards

Chapter 4: Scientific Inquiry	Standards	Standard Reference
Activity 1: Scientific Method	The student should develop: • Abilities necessary to do scientific inquiry • An understanding of scientific inquiry	NS.5-8.1
Activity 2: Famous Scientists	The student should develop an understanding of: • Science and technology • Science as a human endeavor	NS.5-8.6 NS.5-8.7
Chapter 5: Physical Science	**Standards**	**Standard Reference**
Activity 1: Force	The student should develop an understanding of: • Motions and forces	NS.5-8.2
Activity 2: Motion	The student should develop an understanding of: • Motions and forces	NS.5-8.2
Activity 3: Properties of Matter	The student should develop an understanding of: • Properties and changes of properties in matter	NS.5-8.2
Activity 4: Phases of Matter	The student should develop an undertstanding of: • Properties and changes of properties in matter	NS.5-8.2

Activity 5: Acids and Bases	The student should develop an understanding of: • Properties and changes of properties in matter	NS.5-8.2
Activity 6: Using the Periodic Table	The student should develop an understanding of: • Properties and changes of properties in matter	NS.5-8.2
Activity 7: Alternative Energy Sources	The student should develop an understanding of: • Transfer of energy • Science and technology • Science and technology in society	NS.5-8.2 NS.5-8.5 NS.5-8.6
Chapter 6: Earth and Space Science	**Standards**	**Standard Reference**
Activity 1: Types of Rocks	The student should develop an understanding of: • Structure of the earth's system • Earth history	NS.5-8.4
Activity 2: Volcanoes	The student should develop an understanding of: • Structure of the earth's system • Earth history	NS.5-8.4
Activity 3: Minerals	The student should develop an understanding of: • Structure of the earth's system • Earth history	NS.5-8.4
Activity 4: Oceans and Seas	The student should develop an understanding of: • Structure of the earth's system • Earth history	NS.5-8.4
Activity 5: The Solar System	The student should develop an understanding of: • Earth in the solar system	NS.5-8.4
Activity 6: Stars and Galaxies	The student should develop an understanding of: • Earth in the solar system	NS.5-8.4

National Curriculum Standards

Activity 7: The Water Cycle	The student should develop an understanding of: • Structure of the earth's system	NS.5-8.4
Chapter 7: Life Science	**Standards**	**Standard Reference**
Activity 1: Classification of Organisms	The student should develop an understanding of: • Structure and function in living systems	NS.5-8.3
Activity 2: The Structure and Function of Cells	The student should develop an understanding of: • Structure and function in living systems • Regulation and behavior	NS.5-8.3
Activity 3: Cell Division—Mitosis	The student should develop an understanding of: • Structure and function in living systems • Diversity and adaptations of organisms	NS.5-8.3
Activity 4:Cell Division—Meiosis	The student should develop an understanding of: • Structure and function in living systems • Diversity and adaptations of organisms	NS.5-8.3
Activity 5: Heredity and Genetics	The student should develop an understanding of: • Reproduction and heredity • Science and technology • Population, resources, and environment • Risks and benefits • Science and technology in society	NS.5-8.3 NS.5-8.5 NS.5-8.6
Activity 6: Plants	The student should develop an understanding of: • Populations and ecosystems • Diversity and adaptations of organisms • Abilities of technological design • Science and technology • Science and technology in society	NS.5-8.3 NS.5-8.5 NS.5-8.6

Chapter 8: The Human Body	Standards	Standard Reference
Activity 1: The Skeletal System, Joints, and Muscles	The student should develop an understanding of: • Structure and function in living systems • Personal health	NS.5-8.3 NS.5-8.6
Activity 2: The Cardiovascular System	The student should develop an understanding of: • Structure and function in living systems • Personal health	NS.5-8.3 NS.5-8.6
Activity 3: The Central Nervous System	(text tk?)	(text tk?)
Activity 4: The Digestive System	The student should develop an understanding of: • Structure and function in living systems • Personal health	NS.5-8.3 NS.5-8.6
Activity 5: Blood	The student should develop an understanding of: • Structure and function in living systems • Personal health • Risks and benefits • Natural hazards	NS.5-8.3 NS.5-8.6
Activity 6: The Ear	The student should develop an understanding of: • Structure and function in living systems • Personal health • Natural hazards	NS.5-8.3 NS.5-8.6
Activity 7: The Eye	• Structure and function in living systems • Personal health • Natural hazards	NS.5-8.3 NS.5-8.6

Glossary

Acid: any chemical compound that, when dissolved in water, gives a solution with a hydrogen; ion activity greater than in pure water (pH less than 7.0)

Allele: any of the alternate forms of a gene

Amorphous Solid: loses its shape under certain conditions

Anaphase: In anaphase, the spindles are each pulled to opposite ends of the cell. Chromosomes equally divide themselves, having identical features at each end of the cell. Lastly, the cell stretches out to form an oblong shape.

Animals: part of the Eukarya domain

Achaea: found in extreme environments such as hot springs, swamps, ocean floors, salt water, and animal intestines. They are different than bacteria, but still contain cells that have no nucleus.

Arteries: blood vessels that carry blood away from the heart

Asteroid Belt: the space between Mars and Jupiter, separating the inner planets of Mercury, Venus, Earth and Mars from the outer planets

Atomic Mass: bottom number, mass in atomic mass units for all possible isotopes of that element.

Atomic Number: top number, number of protons in one atom

Atrium chambers: receive blood that enters the heart

Axons: carry impulses away from the cells

Bacteria: do not have a nucleus.

Balanced force: equal forces acting on an object in opposite direction

Ball and Socket Joint: allows for the greatest amount of motion, allowing the joint to rotate, twist and turn.

Base: a substance that yields hydroxyl ions when dissolved in water.

Blood types: four major blood types (A, B, AB and O) which are determined by markers. Markers are proteins that are on the red blood cells.

Blue Stars: are very hot stars with short wavelengths and a surface temperatures of almost 30,000 degrees Kelvin

Brain stem: found between the spinal cord and cerebellum controls all of your body's involuntary actions

Cardiac muscle: muscle of the heart. It is considered involuntary.

Cardiovascular system (circulatory system): made up of the heart, blood vessels and blood. Its main job is to carry nutrition and water to all cells and to carry waste products away. It also carries disease preventing materials in the blood that circulate and strengthen the internal organs.

Cell Membrane: outer boundary of the cell, serving as a protective barrier to the nucleus

Cell Wall: strong layer of non-living material that protects the plant cell.

Central Nervous System: consists of the brain and the spinal cord

Cerebellum: second largest area of the brain and controls voluntary muscle movement and balance

Cerebrum: largest area of the brain

Chemical Digestion: food is broken down chemically by acids in the stomach and changes into nutrients and sugars that the body needs in order to survive

Chemical Sedimentary Rocks: formed when the the solids separate from evaporated water (limestone)

Chloroplasts: have chlorophyll which makes food for the plant cells

Cinder Cone Volcanoes: forms a steep sided slope and is made from a single volcanic eruption

Classification System: eight classification levels that scientists use for organisms (domain, kingdom, phyla, class, order, family, genus and species)

Classic Sedimentary: made from bits of rocks and minerals that is compacted (quartz)

Cleavage: the minerals ability to break along even, flat surfaces

Color: many different colors within a mineral

Composite Volcanoes: large, cone like structure that is the product of gaseous magma and generates very viscous lava, with the most explosive eruptions

Condensation: process by which a gas or vapor changes to a liquid

Concave lenses: disseminate the light before focusing on the retina help the problem

Conductive Hearing Loss: occurs when sound vibrations from the tympanic membrane to the inner ear are blocked

Condyloid Joint-: allows movement to occur in smaller areas

Convex lenses: are thick in the middle so light bends inward before reaching the eye.

Cornea: outer shield on the eye

Crystal Form: inside a mineral, a crystal form is visible, forming into well defined faces

Crystalline Solids: made up of crystals and are hard

Cytoplasm: material in the cell that contains the nutrients and water to keep the cell healthy

Decibels: Loudness is measured in units that are called decibels

Dendrites: carry the nerve impulses to the cells

Density: the amount of mass per unit volume of an object

Depth Perception: the ability to judge how near or far objects are in relationship to one another

Deposition: process of a gas turning into a solid

Domains: Bacteria, Achaea, and Eukaryote. Organisms are placed into domains and kingdoms based upon their cell type, the number of cells in their bodies, and their ability to make food for themselves.

Elliptical Galaxies: have no core center or disc. They are an elliptical shape and appear like large spiral patterns of stars.

Endoplasmic Reticulum: moves all nutrients and materials around the cell

Eukaryote: contain a nucleus

Extrusive igneous rocks: formed when the lava cools and hardens (basalt)

Evaporation: conversion of a liquid to the vapor state by the addition of latent heat

Farsightedness: can see far away item very clearly yet close up objects are blurry.

Fluid Friction: when air, water or oil cause resistance between two forces

Foliated Metamorphic Rocks: have been under such extreme conditions that the results of the change in structure cause a rock with a layered appearance

Force: the pushing or pulling on an object

Fossil fuels: also known as mineral fuels, they are hydrocarbon containing natural resources such as coal, petroleum, and natural gas

Fracture: specific ways minerals break When the breakage is uneven, a fracture is said to result

Freezing Point: point that the liquid turns to a solid

Friction: a force that brings an object to rest

Fungi: living vegetable organisms that feed by absorbing nutrients from other organism

Galaxies: large clusters of stars (spiral, elliptical, lenticular and irregular)

Gas: does not have a definite shape or volume

Gene: specific sequence of nucleotides in DNA or RNA that is located usually on a chromosome and that is the functional unit of inheritance controlling the transmission and expression of one or more traits

Geothermal energy: electricity generated by utilizing naturally occurring geological heat sources

Gliding Joint-: allows two smaller and flat bones to move over or on top of one another.

Golgi Bodies: package the proteins in the cell and bring them to the outer parts of the cell

Gravity: the natural force between objects and the earth

Groups or Families: Elements in the same group or family have similar characteristics vertical columns)

Hardness: determined by rubbing a mineral against another mineral

Hemophilia: Hemophilia is a disease of the blood clotting process. It occurs when there is a breakdown in the organization of blood clotting.

Homeostasis: taking in and reporting of information within the CNS system

Hinge joint: moves back and forth

Hydrogen fuel cells: electrochemical cell in which the energy of a reaction between fuel, such as liquid hydrogen, and an oxidant, such as liquid oxygen, is converted into electrical energy **Hydropower:** energy obtained from flowing water

Hydrothermal Solutions-: very hot mixtures of water and dissolve substances that come into contact with existing minerals and change their composition through a chemical reaction

Igneous rock: comes from the cooled magma from volcanic eruptions

Inner Ear: made up of the cochlea, semicircular canal and auditory nerve

Interphase: In this first phase of mitosis, first the cell grows and collects all nutrients to gain strength. Once full grown, the cell begins to copy the DNA found in the nucleus.

Interstellar Matter: space between stars which contains clouds of dust and gases

Intrusive Igneous Rocks: form when the magma cools beneath the earth's surface (Granite)

Iris: controls how much light enters your pupil

Irregular Galaxies: have irregular or different shapes

Joint: a point in the body where two or more bones connect

Lava: molten rock erupting from a volcano that is extremely hot

Lenticular Galaxies: short spiral galaxies that resemble a disk but do not burn hot.

Leukemia: This disease is a form of cancer that involves white blood cells and bone marrow. In leukemia there is an abnormal amount of white blood cells produced.

Light Years: measure the distance light travels in one year

Liquid; is pourable with no definite shape

Luster: minerals shine like metal.

Magma: molten rock formed below the earth's surface

Mass: the amount of matter that is in an object. It is a constant unless the matter itself is altered.

Matter: any substance which has mass and occupies space

Mechanical Digestion: the physical act of breaking down the food we eat

Meiosis: process of cell division where chromosome pairs split and forming new sperm and egg, or sex cells. These sex cells have only half the amount of chromosomes of the parent cell. Reproduction of the species occurs at conception, when the sperm and egg cells unite.

Melting Point: point that the solid changes to a liquid

Metaphase-In this third stage, the chromosomes line up in the middle of the cell and attach to a spindle fiber.

Metamorphic Rocks: igneous or sedimentary rocks that have been changed by heat, water and pressure

The Middle Ear: the tympanic membrane or eardrum picks up the vibrations from the outer ear. Sound waves vibrate on the tympanic membrane similar to that of a drum. In the middle ear there are three tiny, interconnected bones called the hammer, anvil and stirrup.

Minerals: naturally occurring inorganic solids that are found in nature

Mitochondria: breaks down food into energy for the cell

Mitosis: how cells divide

Moveable joint: a joint that allows two bones to move together without damaging one another.

Nearsightedness: have difficulties seeing objects that are far away

Neutral: neither an acid, nor a base, a balance between protons and hydroxide (OH⁻)

Newton's Law #1: An object at rest stays at rest; an object in motion stays in motion unless an unbalanced force acts upon it.

Newton's Law #2: Force equals mass times acceleration.

Newton's Law #3: For every action, there is an equal and opposite reaction

Non-foliated Metamorphic Rocks-: smooth metamorphic rock

Non-moveable joints: bone fibers which bind together to form a joint. Non moveable joints are called saddle joints.

Nonrenewable resource: resources for which there are no ways to replenish the supply (i.e. fossil fuels)

Non-vascular plants: plants that grow on the ground as a ground cover. They do not have roots that feed the rest of the plant structure by absorbing water from the ground.

Nuclear energy: energy released from the nucleus of an atom creating an nuclear reaction

Nuclear Fusion: when stars join together, emitting an energy source that keeps them burning.

Nuclear Membrane: thin structure separates the cell nucleus from the cytoplasm

Nucleus: heart of the cell that houses the DNA and chromosomes

Outer Ear: widest area of the funnel and is designed to gather sound waves

Percolation: movement of water through the rocks, soil and ground that goes back into the lakes, rivers and streams

Periods: Elements in a period are not alike in properties. Atomic size decreases from left to right across a period, but atomic mass increases from left to right across a period. (horizontal rows)

Peripheral nervous system: nerves branching off of the brain and spinal cord

pH: a measure of the acidity or basicity of a solution

Photosynthesis: is the process where green plants use solar energy to convert water, carbon dioxide and minerals into chemical compounds necessary for survival. In simpler terms, this energy is used to make food for the plants.

Plants: make their own food

Plasma: Plasma is made up mostly of water. It carries nutrients, vitamins and minerals to all cells. It also carries waster products away from the cells to be eliminated from the body.

Platelets: parts of cells that look like fibers. They help to form blood clots when cuts or wounds occur.

Precipitation: any form of water that falls to the earth's surface

Presbycusis: occurs because changes occur in the inner ear

Prophase: In this second stage of mitosis, the chromosomes in the nucleus condense and move to opposite sides of the nucleus. Thin spindles form around the chromosomes and form a bridge between both sides of the cell.

Protists: very different from any other, contain nuclei (i.e. seaweed)

Punnett Squares: simple square to show the crossover and probability of an inherited trait.

Pyroclastic Materials: include rocks, glass fragments and debris which are blown out of the volcano

Receptor cells: rods and cones interpret the image. Rod cells work best in the dark or in very dim light. they see mostly blacks, whites and all shades of gray. Cone receptor cells interpret colors and see best in the sunlight. When the light hits the rods and cones, the messages travel to the brain through the optic nerve.

Red Blood Cells: made in your bone marrow. Without red blood cells, your body cannot use oxygen

Red Stars: are cooler stars with longer wavelengths of heat and emit red light. They range in temperature between 2,000-3,500 degrees Kelvin.

Renewable resource: natural resource that is depleted at a rate slower than the rate at which it regenerates (i.e. solar energy)

Ribosomes: make protein for the cell

Rolling Friction: Rolling friction is similar to slide friction. Contact between two surfaces control the motion that is actually created.

Scientific Method: principles and procedures for the systematic pursuit of knowledge involving the recognition and formulation of a problem, the collection of data through observation and experiment, and the formulation and testing of hypotheses

Sedimentary Rocks: formed when solids settle out of a fluid such as water found in oceans or rivers, or air, which then compact together to form sedimentary rocks

Seed plants: have a vascular system and need pollen to reproduce

Sensor neural Hearing Loss: occurs when there is damage to the auditory nerve

Shield Volcanoes: produced from volcanic rock that has hardened from lava and many have grown from the ocean floor and formed islands.

Sickle Cell Anemia: This disease occurs when red blood cells are in the shape of a sickle or a crescent. Because of this shape, blood cells are not flexible and don't travel to all parts of the body very well. Cells then become deprived of oxygen that they need to survive.

Skeletal Muscles: attached to your bone and provide strength. They are voluntary muscles because their movement can be controlled.

Skeletal system: made up of bones, cartilage, tendons and ligaments

Slide Friction: two surfaces glide or slide over each other

Smooth muscles: involuntary and found inside of organs. They move automatically, allowing the systems of the body to function properly

Spiral Galaxies: has a core center or disc that is round and flat and burns very hot and includes interstellar matter

Solar energy: harnessing the energy produced by sunlight

Solid: has a definite shape and volume

Solution: a homogeneous mixture composed of two substances, one dissolved in the other

Stars: light and heat our planet and vary in color depending upon how hot they are. They can be old and young.

Streak: the constant color that the mineral shows when rubbed against an abrasive surface.

Sublimation: the process of solids turning directly into gas

Synapse: electrical impulse

Telephase: In the last phase of cell division called telephase, the chromosomes stretch out and lose their rod-like appearance. A new nucleus is formed at each end of the cell that encases the divided chromosomes. Now, the cell resembles a peanut, and splits in the middle, forming two new, identicaldaughter cells.

Tinnitus: ringing in the ears

Trait: an inherited characteristic

Unbalanced force: 2 forces with different strengths putting a force against each other

Vacuoles: provide storage areas within the cell

Vaporization: process of turning a liquid into vapor

Vascular plants: have tubes in the roots, stems and leaves that nourish the plant with food and water to live and grow

Veins: blood vessels that carry blood back to the heart

Ventricle chambers: pump blood away from the heart

Volcanic Gases: carbon dioxide and sulfur dioxide

Volume: the amount of space occupied by mass measured in liters

Weight: Weight is affected by mass, but it has a variable value. The greater the mass of an object, the greater its pull to the earth or gravitational force.

White Blood Cells: made in the blood marrow. White blood cells are important because they fight disease.

White Stars: very hot stars

Wind power: using the kinetic energy of the wind or wind turbines to extract the wind's energy

Yellow Stars: moderate wavelengths and temperatures. Their range of heat is between 5,000-6,000 degrees Kelvin. An example of a yellow star is the .

Bibliography

Batshaw, M., and Perret, Y. M. *Children with Disabilities—A Medical Primer.* Baltimore: Paul H. Brookes Publishing, 1996.

Brooks, R., and Goldstein, S. *The Power of Resilience.* New York: McGraw-Hill, 2004.

Brown, T. *Attention Deficit Disorder: The Unfocused Mind in Children and Adults.* New Haven: Yale University Press and Wellness, 2006.

Bulgren, J. A, and Schumaker, J. B. *The Paired Associates Strategy-Learning Strategies Curriculum.* Lawrence: University of Kansas Center for Research on Learning, 1996.

Campbell, L., Campbell, B., and Dickinson, D. *Teaching and Learning Through Multiple Intelligences.* (3rd ed.) Boston: Allyn & Bacon, 2003.

Canter, L., and Canter, M. *Succeeding with Difficult Students: New Strategies for Reaching Your Most Challenging Students.* Santa Monica, Calif.: Canter and Associates, 1993.

Coolidge-Stolz, E., et al. *Life Science.* Upper Saddle River, N.J.: Pearson Prentice Hall, 2005.

D'Amico, J., and Drummond, K. *The Science Chef: One Hundred Fun Food Experiments and Recipes for Kids.* Hoboken, N.J.: John Wiley & Sons, 1995.

D'Amico, J., and Drummond, K. *The Science Chef Travels Around the World: Fun Food Experiments and Recipes for Kids.* John Wiley & Sons, 1996.

Deci, E. L. and Flaster, R. *Why We Do What We Do: Understanding Self-Motivation.* New York: Penguin Books, 1996.

Gardner, H. *Multiple Intelligences: The Theory in Practice.* New York: Basic Books, 1993.

Hurd, D., et al. *Physical Science.* Upper Saddle River, N.J.: Pearson Prentice Hall, 1988.

Kahan, P. *Science Explorer: Motion, Forces and Energy.* Upper Saddle River, N.J.: Prentice Hall, 2002.

Lerner, J., and Kline, F. *Learning Disabilities and Related Disorders: Characteristics and Teaching Strategies.* Boston: Houghton-Mifflin, 2005.

Pasachoff, J. M. *Science Explorer: Sound and Light.* Upper Saddle River, N.J.: Prentice Hall, 2002.

Tarbuck, E., and Lutgens, F. *Earth Science.* Upper Saddle River, N.J.: Prentice Hall, 2006.

Yanoff, J. C. *The Classroom Teacher's Inclusion Handbook.* Chicago: Arthur Coyle Press, 2000.

Index

evaluation, 193; for gifted learners, 191; home/school connection for, 193; for learning disabled students, 191; lesson for, 188–189; and national curriculum standards, 228; purpose of, 188; for resistant learners of students with ADD/ADHD, 191; for students with cognitive difficulties, 191; for students with fine motor difficulties, 193; whole class lab for: are you right- or left-brain thinker?, 191–193; worksheet, 190

Cerebellum, 189

Cerebrum, 189

Chemical digestion, 194

Child Study Team, 3–4; checklist for referring student to, 12; collaborating with, 4–12; members of, 6–8; and referral interventions, 8–12

Chloroplasts, 146

Chocolate candy, making (whole class lab), 67

Chromosomes, 146, 221

Cinder cone volcanoes, 95–96

Classic baking soda volcano (whole class lab), 99–100

Classification of organisms activity: answers for, 221; and classification of house cat, 139; evaluation, 144; for gifted learners, 143; home/school connection for, 144; for learning disabled students, 142; lesson for, 138–140; and national curriculum standards, 227; purpose of, 138; for resistant learners or students with ADD/ADHD, 143; for students with physical disabilities, 144; for students with visual difficulties, 142, 144; whole class lab for: making yogurt, 143–144; worksheet, 141

Collaboration: and checklist for prereferral interventions, 5; with Child Study Team, 4–12; effective, 3–16; for intervention, 3–4; with parents and families, 13–15; and prereferral collaboration with school personnel checklist, 9

Commission of the Blind and Visually Impaired, 23

Composite volcanoes, 95

Condensation, 130, 221

Conductive hearing loss, 208, 223

Consultant, 6

Core curriculum standards, 17

Crystalline solid, 63

Cytoplasm, 145

D

Deci, E., 28

Decibels chart, 208, 223

Dendrites, 188

Density, 59, 102, 219

Developmental history, 10

Differentiated learning: and assessing learning styles, 18–19; and differentiated assessment strategies, 29; and effective inclusive classroom, 26–28; and fitting teaching strategies to learners, 21; and identifying intelligence characteristics in middle school classroom, 22; and multiple intelligences and learning strengths, 20–21; and planning for students with special needs, 21–24; preparing for, 17–24; and working with core curriculum standards, 17

Differentiating instruction: effective teaching strategies for, 25–30; and measuring success, 28–29

Digestive system activity: answers for, 223; for delayed readers or students with memory weaknesses, 197; evaluation, 199; for gifted learners, 197; home/school connection for, 198; for learning disabled students, 197; lesson for, 194–195; and national curriculum standards, 228; purpose of, 194; for resistant learners or students with ADD/ADHD, 197;

for students with fine motor or perceptual difficulties, 197, 198; whole class lab for: what is osmosis and what role does it play in digestion, 198; worksheet, 196

DNA (deoxyribonucleic acid), 146; observing (whole class lab), 164

Dyslexia, 23

E

Ear activity: answers for, 223; evaluation, 212; for gifted learners, 210; home/school connection for, 212; for learning disabled students, 210; lesson for, 207–208; and national curriculum standards, 228; purpose of, 207; for resistant learners and students with ADD/ADHD, 210, 211; for students with fine motor or perceptual difficulties, 211; for students with memory weakness, 210; for students with perceptual difficulties, 210; for students with physical difficulties, 211; whole class lab for: organized sound, 211; worksheet, 209

Earth, 116

Earth and space science: and minerals, 101–106; and oceans and seas, 107–114; and solar system, 115–122; and stars and galaxies, 123–128; and types of rocks, 86–94; and volcanoes, 95–100; and water cycle, 129–135

Edible cell division (whole class lab), 158–159

Educational evaluation, 10

Educational Therapist (LDT/C), 6, 10

Elliptical galaxies, 124

Endoplasmic reticulum, 145

English as a Second Language services, 10

Esophagus, 195, 197, 223

Eukarya, 139

Evaporation, 130

Eye activity: answers for, 223–224; evaluation, 218; for gifted learners, 218; home/school connection for, 218; for learning disabled students, 217; lesson for, 213–215; and national curriculum standards, 228; purpose of, 213; for students with ADD/ADHD, 217; for students with cognitive difficulties, 217; for students with memory weakness, 217; for students with physical disabilities, 218; whole class lab for: is vision our most precious sense?, 218; worksheet, 216

F

Famous scientists activity: evaluation, 44; home/school connection for, 43; lesson for, 40; national curriculum standards for, 225; purpose of, 40; table for, 41; whole class lab for: scientific contributions, 43–44; worksheet for, 42

Farsightedness, 214–215

504 Plan, 23–24

Fluid friction, 46

Force activity: answers for, 219; for delayed readers, 49–50; evaluation for, 51; for gifted learners, 50; home/school connection for, 51; lesson for, 46–47; and national curriculum standards, 225; purpose of, 46; for students with cognitive difficulties, 49; whole class lab for: tug of war, 51; worksheet, 48

Fossil fuels, 82, 220

Friction, 46

Fungi, 140, 221

Funny putty, making (whole class lab), 38

G

Gardner, H., 20, 21

Gases, 63, 64, 96, 220

GEMS Alien Juice Bar, 72